TALES FROM THE GRAVE:
AN ANTHOLOGY OF TRUE GHOST STORIES

EDITED BY
R. G. NOJEK

Rainstorm Press
PO BOX 391038
Anza, Ca 92539
www.RainstormPress.com

ISBN 13 – 978-1-937758-14-1

Interior design by –
The Mad Formatter
www.TheMadFormatter.com

Front cover illustration by Mike Payne
Mikepdp@hotmail.co.uk

This book is for Tina, thank-you for being a mother to my sister and me.

TABLE OF CONTENTS

MY LIFE WITH THE DEAD
KRISTINA R. MOSLEY

It was the middle of May, and it was starting to get warm. I sat on the edge of the narrow school bus seat, trying not to let my duffel and sleeping bag push me into the aisle. I stared out the front window, ready to get to Camp Tahkodah.

The camp belonged to a local Christian university, but the school rented it out when it wasn't used in the summer. My elementary school employed the trip to the camp as a reward for a year of good behavior. Since I was always quiet and well behaved, I got to go.

I spent the roughly forty-minute trip wondering what my time at the camp would be like. I had never been camping at all in my eleven years, nor had I been to a summer camp. I knew that none of the teachers or students would be in tents because Camp Tahkodah had multiple cabins with beds in them. There was also a bathroom in each cabin. I wouldn't exactly be roughing it. Additionally, it was just an overnight trip. I doubted very much would happen.

I was wrong.

On the way, one of the teachers called out cabin assignments. I was to be in Cabin Three. That was fine, but I didn't really care for the other girls in the cabin. Our cabin chaperone was an aide for the special education teacher, so I didn't know her at all. I didn't like anything that was happening.

The other students seemed excited when we reached the camp. They shouted and ran around. A different emotion filled me; it was a feeling that wasn't quite dread. The trip was the first time I was away from both of my parents. I was stuck in a cabin with people I didn't really know. I was too shy to be particularly friendly to anyone. I suspected that I wasn't going to have much fun at Camp Tahkodah.

I entered Cabin Three so I could put away my things. Names and dates of kids who had stayed in the cabin in previous years covered the walls of the first room. This room had four sets of bunk beds. There were two built-in cabinets where we could put our belongings, along with an old white chest of drawers. I walked over to the cabinet furthest from the door and stuck my black duffel bag inside.

I walked through the rest of the cabin. There were no interior doors, so an empty doorway led to the second, smaller room that had three sets of bunk beds and another chest of drawers. On the other side of the wall was the bathroom. An old shower curtain covered the doorway for privacy. The room was just a toilet, a sink with a mirror above it, and a shower. It was all pretty basic, but nothing horrible.

I went back to the front of the cabin to choose my bed, deciding on one to the right side of the cabin, closest to the door. Then, I climbed up to the top bunk and placed my borrowed burgundy and dark blue sleeping bag on the bed. I still don't know what possessed me to pick the top bed. I was afraid of any kind of height, still am. Maybe I wanted to try something new since I'd never slept in a bed that high before. More likely, though, I was subconsciously isolating myself from the other girls, who had commandeered the middle room. I wanted to be as far away from them as possible. Soon, our chaperone ushered us out of the cabin.

Sometime during the camping activities of hiking, making tie-dyed shirts, playing in the water, and learning about weather patterns, (it was a school trip, after all) I overheard a conversation. One of the sixth grade girls spoke to one of my fifth grade classmates.

"Did you hear about Elizabeth?" the older girl asked.

"No, who's that?"

"Elizabeth was a camp counselor here a long time ago. Her boyfriend was, too. Anyway, he killed her and chopped her up. He threw the pieces in the cabins. Cabin Three got a lot of the pieces, but Cabin Nine got the most. Now, Elizabeth haunts the camp."

Conflicting feelings of belief and disbelief fought inside my head. On one hand, the story lacked details that would make it more believable. Also, the only ghost stories I had heard had been in books. They were either complete works of fiction or happened to other people. I had never seen a ghost, so why should I have believed in one? On the other hand, just because I'd never seen a ghost didn't mean a person couldn't become one. There were billions of people in the world who existed even if I never met them. The moon didn't stop being in the sky during the day just because I didn't see it.

I was still more doubtful than anything else. I had never believed in Santa, and he seemed more likely to me than a ghost. So, I went about my business, wanting the trip to be over. I wandered around the camp and saw a group of kids gathered outside Cabin Nine. One of the students was my former neighbor, Nicole. She held a pencil and a piece of paper.

"What are you doing?" I asked.

"We're writing a letter to Elizabeth," she said, looking around at the group. "We're gonna tell her that we're sorry she's dead so she won't hurt us."

"Do you believe the story?"

Another girl spoke up. "Someone wrote the words 'get out' over and over in Cabin Nine."

I remembered the sixth-grader's story. I remembered how most of Elizabeth's remains were supposed to be in Cabin Nine. The messages from past campers pointed to the fact that something had happened there. I also remembered that, according to the story, Elizabeth's boyfriend threw many of her parts in Cabin Three, my cabin.

"Could you put my name on that, too?" I asked. Better safe than sorry, I thought.

"Yeah, sure," Nicole replied. She scribbled my name at the end of the letter with the names of the other campers.

After a few minutes, I wandered away, trying to decide if I actually believed the story. I felt a bit more concerned after talking to the other kids. I think their fear worsened my own. It was like I was justified. If they weren't afraid, I could easily explain my feelings away as the products of a worrisome mind. However, if other people believed a ghost haunted the ground of Camp Tahkodah, then there must have been one.

Being a kid, though, the fear or whatever it was floated to the back of my mind, my self-imposed isolation replacing it. My friends weren't extremely close, personally, and I couldn't muster up the courage or even the willpower to talk to anyone else. I ambled around the camp, drinking from a juice pouch, while waiting for the next activity.

That night, after a dinner of hot dogs and smores, we played hide and seek in the dark. I actually had fun. Sneaking around in the dark was one of the things at which I excelled. No one who was "it" managed to tag me. After a while, though, I got bored of just running around, and I decided to walk back to the cabin. The way was dark, but I wasn't concerned with what could have been lurking in the night. To me, Elizabeth was just a story.

When I got back to the cabin, I took a shower. I didn't notice earlier that there was a gap between the bathroom wall and the ceiling. The girls in the middle room sat on the top bunk of the bed that was against the wall and threatened to peek over at me. This was quite possibly the worst thing a prudish, chubby girl with self-esteem issues like me could hear. I yelled at them and got out of the shower as quickly as I could.

I got in bed and tried to go to sleep, but the other girls thought differently. They wanted to stay up as long as they could and be raucous kids. Another girl on the other side of the room wanted to go to bed as well, and the girls gave her a hard time. I don't know why they didn't mess with me. Maybe it was because the other girl was whinier than I was. I looked to the teacher, expecting her to say something. She was asleep. Frustrated, I told the girls to stop, or something to that extent, and turned over.

That night, I woke up repeatedly. Sometimes, I would go to the bathroom, turning on the light in the middle room. I doubted I made any friends with the girls in the room, but I was still mad at them. Then, I would go back to my bed and return to a fitful slumber.

I opened my eyes for what must have been the fifth or sixth time. I wondered what time it was, because the cabin was still dark. A sliver of light from a lamp outside provided just enough illumination for me to see the doorway leading to the rest of the cabin. As I was about to turn over and go back to sleep, something at the back of the building caught my attention. It's just someone coming back from the bathroom, I thought.

It couldn't have been, though, unless one of the girls had learned to levitate. The figure floated toward me, and I saw that it was a luminous misty green, roughly the same color as a sea foam green crayon. The apparition moved closer. It was a woman wearing a long, flowing dress. She held something large and round in her hands.

Is that her head? I wondered.

I didn't want to find out. I did the only thing I knew to do: I hid. I shut my eyes as tightly as I could and pulled my sleeping bag over my head. Sleep soon reclaimed me.

My eyes didn't open again until the morning. I was exhausted, far more tired than I was when I went to sleep the night before. I felt completely drained of energy. My head was light and my chest was heavy. What's wrong with me? I wondered.

I climbed off the top bunk. On the way down, I noticed a large black bruise on my left forearm, next to the elbow. I thought I had just bumped it getting in and out of bed in the night. Must've hit it pretty hard, I mused. Then, I noticed my other injury. Something had scratched a capital E into my arm, right in the middle of the bruise. The scratches were deep enough to bleed because there were dark scabs over the cuts.

Looking at my arm again, I realized the E was the main injury and the angry bruise was like a byproduct. Whatever attacked me was strong.

This wasn't from climbing, I decided. I doubted any of the people in Cabin Three hurt me. We were all ten- and eleven-year-old girls. Surely, none of them was that warped. While I was a sound sleeper, someone cutting me with that much force would wake me. The most damning evidence to me, however, was that the E faced me. If one of the girls were the assailant, her climbing on the bed would've jarred me from sleep. Even if my left arm had been hanging off the side of the bed, I doubt a kid would have enough foresight to cut properly.

That E was for Elizabeth; I knew it. The thing I saw the night before wasn't a dream or a figment of my imagination. It was an actual ghost. Why did she attack me, though? Everyone in my cabin had heard the story. Was it because I was awake? Was it because I was on the fence about believing the story? If that were the case, she sure convinced me.

Strangely, I didn't think to tell anyone about what happened to me. It was probably for the best, though. No one would believe the story, most likely. Worse, they might have thought the wound was self-inflicted and that maybe I made up the whole thing for attention.

The rest of the day passed in a fog. I picked at breakfast and lunch, and I sat on a bench rather than run around with the rest of the kids. I was too exhausted to do anything else. I counted down the hours until I could go home and be away from Camp Tahkodah forever. I finally arrived home, where I slept for seventeen hours straight.

When the next year came along, I was once again well behaved enough to be able to return to Camp Tahkodah. Luckily, my school allowed students to miss school without penalty if they qualified but didn't want to go on the good behavior field trip. I chose to stay home those two days. I told anyone who asked that it was because I didn't have fun the year before. This was true. A ghost attack kind of ruins the fun of camp.

* * *

The next seven years of my life went by fairly normally. Well, ghost-free, anyway. In August 2005, I began attending Arkansas Tech University. People have reported numerous incidents of paranormal activity. Some of these stories included a piano playing by itself in a music practice room or a basketball bouncing in the gym when no one was around. Those aren't my stories, though.

The university's housing department assigned me to Caraway Hall, a residence hall with its own haunted history. According to legend, a girl hanged herself from one of the second story windows. After her death, the school bricked up the window and turned the room into two, much smaller rooms. Later, there were reports of strange noises and sightings.

I knew about some of these stories because my sister lived in Caraway when she started at Tech eleven years earlier. I was doubtful, though. Even after my encounter with Elizabeth, I was skeptical. I was open to the idea of the paranormal, but I needed to experience things myself.

The first thing I noticed when I arrived at the dorm was an overwhelming feeling of sadness, as if something horrible happened in the building. I hadn't noticed it while visiting my sister when she lived there. The feeling intensified when I reached my tiny dorm room. The walls were pale green, one of the beds was broken, and there was only one desk. Because of the sad feeling and the room's inadequacy, I wasn't sure how I could live in the room all year.

I assumed the feeling would go away in a few days after I got used to things. The only time it diminished was when I was away from my room. Everything would be fine when I was in class or at the cafeteria or visiting my brother at his building, but once I returned to Caraway, that spooky feeling returned. (It didn't help that the building had attic windows similar to the Amityville Horror house. At night, they looked like eyes glowing in the darkness.)

After a few days, I learned that I lived in the haunted room. I had suspected as much when I noticed the bricked up window at the front of the building. Also, the room across the hall was larger than mine. I assumed that my room was bigger before the girl killed herself, but I read stories online that the university had the room across the hall expanded to accommodate extra students. For a time, my room was closed and used as storage, but as the university grew, students needed the room.

The news of my room's alleged haunted status didn't faze me, but, after a ghost attack, nothing much did. Other than the sadness, everything else was normal. My roommate and I got along all right. The people on my particular wing weren't overly loud. I didn't think there was a ghost in my room because I saw no proof of one.

Things changed after I had lived in Caraway Hall for approximately a week. I was returning from the community showers one night. My roommate was already asleep, so the door to my room was locked. I set my shower caddy on the gray carpet and fumbled in my robe pocket for my keys. I pulled them out and found the one for the door.

"Hey," a girl said behind me.

I tried not to show my surprise as I turned. A dark-haired girl and a blonde girl stood in the hallway. I recognized them as freshmen from orientation sessions we had during move-in weekend. "Hey," I replied. What do they want? I wondered.

"This is the haunted room, right?" the dark-haired girl asked.

"It's supposed to be," I said quickly, trying to get rid of them.

"Anything weird happen?" the blonde asked.

"Not that I know of."

The dark-haired spoke again. "Can we come in and see?"

I knew I shouldn't have let them in. My roommate was asleep. I knew that I would be angry if the situations were reversed and strangers woke me up. Plus, frankly, my room wasn't any of their business. I also knew, however, that I was extremely passive then, and, to me, the easiest way to make them go away was just to let them look.

"Okay," I said, "but be quiet. My roommate's asleep."

I unlocked the door and turned on the light. My roommate stirred in her bed, but she didn't wake up. The girls stepped into the room and looked around. I guess they were satisfied, because they soon left. I went to bed not too long after.

It's funny how the universe works. Up until I talked to the girls about it, nothing strange had happened in my room other than the sadness. The next day, though, things went awry.

I came into the room between classes and tried to use the phone. There was no dial tone, just a faint buzz. I didn't think much of it because there had been repairmen in and out of the building since I had been there. Little was working properly when I moved in: the new washers and dryers weren't functional. The recently remodeled bathrooms still had some issues. Therefore, I thought that someone was just working on the telephone line. I went on my way. I returned to my room after my last class of the day to discover water leaking from the ceiling, spilling onto the tile floor.

Instead of contacting my resident assistant like a logical human, I freaked out and went to my brother's room in a building on the other side of campus. I used his phone to call our mom, who told me to contact someone who could actually do something about it.

I can't remember if I contacted an RA or if my roommate came back, discovered the room, and informed someone. Anyway, an RA told us that a pipe in the ceiling burst and that we should pack up all of our things. Then, we were given the options of either going to overflow, which was the collection of hotel rooms the university rented for the superfluous students that couldn't be placed in housing, or one of us could move to a room in Turner Hall, a co-ed residence hall. My roommate decided to go to overflow, and I chose to move to Turner because my brother lived there. At least I would know someone else in my building.

Later, my roommate and I were packing our things so we could go to the new places. The door was open, and one of our neighbors stuck her blonde head in.

"What happened?" she asked.

"A pipe in the ceiling busted," my roommate said.

The neighbor nodded knowingly. "I lived in here last year, and the ceiling leaked. It was so horrible that I didn't want to live in the room again."

We muttered our acknowledgement. The girl wished us luck and returned to her room.

My roommate and I returned to packing. She opened her closet door and made a sound of frustration, something that was a cross between a grunt and a sigh.

"What's going on?" I asked.

"My clothes got wet."

"That sucks."

"Are your clothes wet?"

I checked. "No, mine are all dry."

"That's weird," she muttered.

Yeah, it is, I thought. My roommate's closet was all the way by the door, while my closet was located behind the spot in the ceiling from which the water leaked. It didn't make sense, but I didn't question it. I was thankful that at least one thing was going right that day.

After a few hours, I got the rest of my things packed and some of the housing staff took me over to

Turner Hall. It was close to midnight by this point, so I found my showering supplies and my clothes for the next day. The new place was unfamiliar to a disorienting degree. I had to relearn everything: where the bathroom was, where the laundry room was, how to get to my classes from Turner. Despite all of this, I immediately felt more welcome than I did at Caraway. I didn't feel the sadness anymore.

The next day, I met my new roommate while I unpacked my belongings. She seemed okay, but it turned out she was a different kind of "ghost roommate." She lived off-campus with her boyfriend, essentially, so she was never in the room. This worked just fine for me.

A few weeks later, my sister visited me at school, and we discussed what happened when I lived in Caraway. She had never told me much about any paranormal activity she might have heard about while she lived at Caraway. She talked about random noises, but she probably thought it was just the building settling. Well, she wanted to know exactly what happened when I lived in the haunted room. I explained everything to her.

"I heard stories about the pipes busting before I lived there," she said. "Rust from the pipes got on everything. That's why it was storage for a while."

"Thanks for telling me," I replied sarcastically.

"I couldn't remember which room was supposed to be haunted."

Soon, I put my time at Caraway behind me, and I lived my entire college career in Turner. It wasn't the newest or nicest place, but at least it wasn't haunted.

Could the whole thing have been a coincidence? Absolutely. The building was old, built in the 1930s, I believe. What was the likelihood, though, that the same pipe would burst in the same room year after year? The third floor bathroom was above my room, but surely, someone could've found a way to keep the pipes intact.

The strangest part of the whole situation to me was the fact that my clothes didn't get wet when my closet was so close to the leak, yet my roommate's did. I still joke that it was because the ghost in Caraway liked me better. Maybe she knew that I had an encounter with one of her kind. I made it through that, so I was an okay person. Yeah, maybe that's it. Or maybe I'm just full of it, and the whole thing was happenstance.

* * *

Most people never come across anything that they could consider paranormal. Few of those that do have more than one experience in their lifetimes. I don't know why I had to share two parts of my life with the dead. Was I an easy target for Elizabeth? Did the Caraway ghost sense my loneliness as I had sensed hers and find in me a kindred spirit, as it were? I don't know. I hope I never do, honestly. Two ghostly encounters in one lifetime are plenty.

SNEAK
LISAMARIE LAMB

It was a seeping, creeping horror that sneaked beneath the bedclothes and lay down with me in the dead of night, in the cold, close darkness. I shivered and waited for it, knowing it would come, knowing it would find me, and I could do nothing except let it engulf me entirely.

For two years, I didn't sleep very much. Not if I was in that room. Not if I was on my own. And even when I did have company he, she, or it, was never far away. I knew that. I could feel it as it watched, lurking in the corner (always *that* corner, the one by the window, where I had first seen it), until it was night, and then it would slink on spiny tiptoes to the side of my bed and stand, watching, until dawn.

I never saw it. Not clearly. Not really. I wonder if I wanted to or whether I was happier knowing but not knowing. Not knowing what it really was. Who it had been, once upon a time.

It was the fear that was the worst. Long, drawn out breaths of shaking terror. The days were fine at first. The days were good in the beginning. In the daytime, I forgot. But as the night drew in, as I readied myself for bed and found as many excuses as I could not to go, I remembered. And then, of course, later, when it became bored of waiting, I would sense it in the light too.

And it wasn't just me. Not at the end.

But let's go back to the beginning.

We were moving. It was decided. I was nine and so

too young to know why, or really care. The only thing I was worried about was finding a big bedroom, bigger than the one I already had, and a garden that I could run around in. I wanted these things even though I loved my bedroom and its cosy smallness, and even though I was not the sort of child who ever ran. It didn't matter. It was exciting and interesting and I would be getting a new house. Even though I didn't think, there was anything wrong with the old one.

I don't remember any of the houses we viewed. None at all. Except for that one. The one we – my parents – bought. That house. The house I grew to love and despise equally. The house in which my biggest fears and fondest memories reside. The house I still say, still believe, was the best house I ever lived in, despite everything. The house I'm still looking for now, a replica of it, my own little reminder of home.

It was very middle class. A four bedroom detached house on a quiet, sought after, road, and walking distance to the station. It had a paved driveway and an integral garage and was old but not that old. 1950s. Built just after the war and as sturdy as Churchill.

It was sunny on the day we first viewed it. Sunny and warm and it must have been nearing the end of summer because we moved in on 5th November of that year. But being nine, I took no notice of days and dates. Why should I have? There's enough time to worry about calendars when you're old. But whatever the date, whatever the season, it was warm and pleasant. We strolled down to the bottom of the one hundred foot garden, and I remember the trees. Enormous evergreens that flanked both sides of the garden, guarding us from the neighbours, from everything. I loved them.

And, we walked down the garden, and then, as there was not much more to see, we walked up again.

It was as we neared the house that I saw it for the first time. Just me. Only me. I had glanced up at the house and there, in the window on the landing, just where the stairs bent round and back on themselves, was a figure. A person. Watching us. And I, as children tend to do, turned excitedly and pointed backwards; "There's someone in the house! On the landing!"

My parents followed my trembling finger. They stared. "I can't see anyone," said my mother. "The house is empty."

This was indeed true. The house was a vacant possession. It was unfurnished and dusty and the mice may or may not have been nibbling at the electrics. And yet, there had been someone standing on the stairs. There had been someone looking out of the window.

"I saw them," I mumbled, embarrassed and confused.

My father looked to the estate agent, and then; "What did they look like?"

But I couldn't say. I couldn't put it into words. They – it? – didn't look like anything. Just a vague outline and a misremembered face. A man, I thought. In a suit. But maybe not. I shrugged. My parents, thinking, I assume, that I was playing some strange game, dismissed it. Then. But the estate agent... Did I see a flash in his eyes? Did I see worry cloud over him? Just for an instant? I believe now that he knew. Something. That he was aware of something and that I had frightened him.

I'm sorry for that.

But I wish he had spoken his fears aloud.

Even though I doubt it would have made any difference. We all loved the house, even me, perhaps especially me, and so we bought it. My parents bought it. And there were no more strangers staring, no more figures floating around. It was just us, the four of us, and that was good.

My sister, the fourth member of the family, had the room at the front of the house, the one with the enormous eaves cupboard where my father built a huge shelf to house all of her dolls and bears and cuddly things. It was a nice room, a comfortable room, and a fair size.

My parents had the room next door, also looking out over the front, out onto the driveway and the road. Again, a good room, twice the size of my sister's and eventually they installed an ensuite shower room and fitted cupboards. Quite right.

But my room was the only one that looked out over the back garden.

It was a big room.

It was light and airy, bright and creamy walled, with a basin in the corner and a row of white wardrobes – four of them - full of shelves and rails, more storage than I needed, but the idea of filling these spaces with things, *any* things, books or toys or clothes... It was magical. That's how I described it to my school friends. *I now live in a magical house. It's the biggest house with the biggest garden I have ever seen. I will live there always. And I think it might have a secret passage.*

Why I thought that I can't remember. But I did

spend a lot of time knocking on walls, convincing myself that I could hear the hollowness behind them, that all I needed to do was break through the old wallpaper and the plaster and there would be that passage. It would probably lead down, below the house, and it would probably take me to an underground city. Probably.

The walls definitely sounded hollow.

The haunting – because that's what it so obviously was – did not start straight away. I couldn't say whether we'd been in the house for weeks or months when my father started to knock down the wall, tiny, made of odd shaped rocks, that separated the garden from the pavement outside. The neck of the driveway was just a little too narrow, and taking away a couple of the stones from that end would help guide the cars in more easily.

I watched him as he swung the pickaxe, smacking the stone, dislodging it, moving it to one side. I was so intent on watching him that I failed to notice the woman, tweed suit and a hat, who had walked up to him and stood, waiting.

"Can I help you?" asked my father.

The woman crossed her arms, clearly irritated. And then she told the story of that wall. Every house in the crescent had one, and the stones were part of the old main house that had stood on this ground many a year back, before the war. The owner had sold the land to build houses for the soldiers of the area when they returned or their families if they didn't. A good thing. A kind thing. And the wall was not to be removed. "We don't want to lower the tone of the neighbourhood," said the woman as she walked away, her job done.

But it was too late. Although the wall was still standing, two stones at the end had been moved, taken into the back garden and laid on a patch of earth that was destined to become a rockery.

But no one would notice. Would they?

Things changed after that. I have no dates, no times, but the change came about gradually, that I *do* know. The sneaking fear crept up almost unnoticed. It began with a strange dream, something vaguely remembered about an angry man dying alone, an evil man who had done terrible things, but none of them explicitly explained. And a child. No face, just a sad voice crying out in the night. Then it took a little longer for me to go to sleep. No matter how tired I was I would lie there, staring at the artexed ceiling, yawning and waiting to nod off. After a while, when I did finally sleep, I would awake in the night, shivering, too scared to move. Little things, gently moving me towards terror. Eventually, the fear became a real thing, tangible, suffocating the joy out of me, punishing me for some unknown slight. And finally there was no sleep. I no longer stared at the ceiling, my eyes were closed against the terrible thing that was stalking me, but I could see the sun rising behind my eyelids, and only then would I sleep.

I am curious about the delay, as though the ghost was waiting to see what we were like, judging our worth. What was it that we, or more accurately I, did to anger this ghost? To make it so wrathful that it had to bully a nine year old who didn't understand and who simply wanted it to go away? I still wonder. I'd like to have apologised, but it never gave me the chance.

Instead it clearly disliked me.

And as I tried to sleep in my haunted bedroom, as I lay there, eyes scrunched closed, still as stone, too afraid to look because I knew, really knew, that there was a thing, a truly unhappy and livid non-living thing, standing beside me, or lying next to me, or hovering above me, I thought I might die. I believed it. The fear was so intense that I knew sometimes that I wasn't breathing anymore. And despite knowing this, and knowing that I had to breathe, understanding all of that, I couldn't do it. It was as though the terror of the night had paralysed me, had wrapped itself around me, and was refusing to let me go.

At first it was just me. I was the only one who had seen it the day of the viewing, and maybe it focused on me for that reason. But I was an easy target, and it had done what it needed to do. It had taken my love for that house and broken it to pieces. It had shown me that there was more than I had ever imagined there could be, that there was life after death, and that it was not all good. So it moved on. Onwards and upwards and into the light of the day.

I was living now in a sort of permanent on edge state, jumpy and on the verge of tears, not wanting to do anything for fear of upsetting that thing that hated me. Any unexpected sound – and some expected ones – set me shaking. Being alone, at home, at school, at a friend's house, would send me running to find company, sure that something – one thing in particular - was coming to get me. I hardly dared look in a mirror for fear that I would see something other than myself. And the garden, too, became a place of fear.

Because from the garden I could see the house. I could see the landing window. And I might see the ghost again.

It was the voices that persuaded my mother. I could hear them, a whispering murmur, nothing concrete, no actual words as far as I could tell, but definitely a conversation going on. I don't believe I was supposed to hear it. I think I was supposed to be aware of it, but nothing more than that. But it was daytime, it was the summer, and those voices should not be happening. I ran to my mother, dragged her up the stairs from the kitchen where she had been making lunch, and I made her listen.

It took a little while.

It took time for her ears to become accustomed to my ghostly nemesis. And his companion. But then she looked at me, her eyes wide, her hand flying to her mouth. And both of us, numb with dread, raced from the room and downstairs and we said nothing.

The whispering had not followed us and for that we were grateful.

My mother, being the braver one, said she was going back upstairs, said she had to listen again, had to know more. I followed, reluctant to stay downstairs by myself in case it was a trap and this was how it planned to finish me.

The room was in pieces. My books, my toys, my clothes, whatever else had been in my magical wardrobes, were now on the floor, flung about as though a whirlwind had passed through the house. Nothing else was touched. My bed was neatly made, my desk was tidy. But the wardrobes had spewed forth everything else that I owned and the doors were left hanging open, swaying.

I slept in my parents' room that night.

I slept there, on a mattress on the floor, for many nights to come.

My father, practical, seemingly fearless, decided that, since the big room at the back was no longer being used, he would take it for an office. He had just started his own business, and needed a place to work. It was perfect. And I, eventually, when I felt I could manage to be alone at night again, moved into the small spare room, just enough space for a desk and a bed and a skinny chest of drawers.

No room for a ghost.

And I was untroubled for a while.

I could sleep again and my father had a space large enough for his computers and faxes and printers and shelves and shelves of folders.

But the ghost was not gone.

I could still feel him, I still knew he was watching.

But now we had another one to deal with.

The man was no face was waiting for something, I knew. And he still scared me, although as I came to realise he had got his wish and I was no longer in what I assumed was his room, I began to relax. And I began to love the house again. My fear subsided and I was able to be on my own once more. I no longer felt watched. I could sleep.

The little blonde girl in the white nightgown who took the man's place didn't worry me. Perhaps I had used all my fear up. Perhaps I had just seen and felt worse. But whatever the reason, when I first saw her I simply kept walking. It was only minutes later that my mind reminded me of what I had just seen, and I rushed back to the scene of the visitation. But she was, of course, gone.

It was that room again.

That's where I first saw her.

I walked past, and the door was open. I glanced in and there, standing at the basin in the corner, brushing her long, blonde hair, beautiful, shiny hair, was the little girl. Wearing a white nightgown, long, down to her dainty feet, long sleeved too, with lace ruffles at the wrists, she was studying herself in a mirror that wasn't there.

And I just kept on walking, to my sister's room, ignoring what I had seen until later.

That was the first and only time I ever saw her.

My mother saw her twice more.

The first time, my mother was walking up the garden after tending to the vegetables she had planted further down. We had a hamster then, a strange, silly little thing called Primrose, and on sunny days my mother would place her cage outside. The cage sat on our garden table, on the patio just outside the kitchen window. Primrose loved the sun's rays on her furry little body and I still believe her daily dose of fresh air is the reason she lived to the old age that she did.

But on this occasion, there was someone standing by the cage, her back to my mother, peering in, seemingly fascinated by the little creature inside. The long, white nightgown and the long blonde hair would have been familiar to me, but my mother thought a stranger had wandered in from the street, through the back gate. If it had been an adult, my mother might have reacted differently, but this was a little girl, in her bedclothes. "Lovely, isn't she?" my mother called towards her strange visitor, wanting her to know she was there, wanting her to know she had been spotted. "She's called Primrose."

The girl turned, and she smiled. Sweet, angelic.

My mother stopped walking. It wasn't right, she said. It was just not quite real.

And when the girl vanished, leaving my mother staring open-mouthed at the hamster's cage sitting placidly on the table, her feeling was proved correct. A ghost. There was no other answer.

It was starting again.

But the girl was not malevolent. She was just there, curious about us, as much as we were about her.

She was shy, though. And she only appeared once more.

The next time, the last time, anyone saw her, the girl was sitting on the stairs, still in her nightgown, peering through the banister rails, watching my mother as she baked something or other in the kitchen. Sensing something, my mother looked up and saw her. That raised a smile from the both of them, just an acknowledgement, no harm meant.

But then the man appeared. That man. Back again. He appeared in the hallway at the bottom of the stairs and the girl disappeared, never to return. And when he turned to look at my mother, he did not smile.

And then she was left alone, shaken, scared to move. Wondering what she – and the girl – had done wrong.

He was nasty, that man.

He was angry at everything and everyone now, not just me.

Any time anything was changed in the house he

threw a tantrum. He particularly liked stamping up the stairs in the dead of night, pausing outside bedroom doors and then walking away again. Threatening.

Only once did he cause physical hurt. My grandmother was working in my father's new office when it happened. Working in the house had become problematic, with my father working too many hours, the office being too convenient. And so to combat this he refurbished the mostly unused garage. He turned it into a separate office which could be locked at night and forgotten about until morning.

The male ghost was obviously not keen on this idea.

My grandmother was stepping out of the garage, one foot on the ground outside, one still on the step, when he pushed her. He slammed into her back and she fell, sprawling down onto the jagged stones on the pebbled path, her head smashing against the stones, her ankle twisting.

She bled a lot.

She bruised a lot.

And she knew she had been pushed.

We tried to tell her that she was wrong, that she had slipped or tripped or stumbled somehow. But she was adamant. There had been hands, strong, tough, large hands, on her back, and they had pushed with a raging force, intending to see her down to the ground.

We didn't want to believe her.

But we did. We had to.

It was him. That man. And now he was dangerous. Now we had proof of it.

My sister, bravest of us all, had taken the opportunity to expand her territory when my father's office moved out to the garage. She immediately took my old room, the room in which this all began. The room into which I hardly dared to step foot for fear of what would happen to me, for fear of what I would see.

She never heard or saw a thing.

She was lucky.

She was also Take That's biggest fan and she spent many an hour decorating that room from floor to ceiling (and even across the ceiling) in posters of the group. Even that didn't raise the ire of the ghost, although it did intrigue us all and we – excluding me – would often enter the room just to admire my sister's handiwork. It was impressive. I have photos of it and cannot see a single spot of the cream coloured wall behind the posters.

My mother and grandmother were in there one day. They were just chatting, talking about this and that and nothing really, when the whispering began again. Urgent, rushed, angry and violent, a male voice saying something but the words couldn't be made out, it was too concentrated, too hurled together. A continuous stream of sound that should have meant something. That could have meant anything.

And then there was one word, said in a plaintive, child's voice, louder than anything else, but so lost, so scared that it pained both my mother and grandmother to the point of tears; "Mummy."

Again, it came; "Mummy."

Silence followed, but the air became thick with menace and violence. My grandmother couldn't move. Her feet were stuck to the bright carpet, her legs unable to move, and she felt sick and dizzy, broken and so scared. My mother, fearing for her own mother's well-being, perhaps, even, her life, dragged her from the room and they collapsed together on the landing, the air sweet and light again, the fury gone.

But that poor little girl.

Whatever became of her?

We moved not long after that. We left that wonderful, terrible house, and I miss it still, even with its previous occupants and their strange, unknown story.

The man was pleased, I'm sure. On the last night in the house, surrounded by boxes and the haunting echoes of an emptying house, my mother could not sleep. It was too warm, even though it was December, and she was unsettled. She got out of bed and went to the window, perhaps simply wanting to take a last, long look at a view she had known for seven years but had never really studied.

And there, beneath the lamppost on the street outside, stood the man. He stamped his feet and rubbed his hands together and could have been anyone. But it wasn't anyone. It was him. And he knew my mother had seen him. I think he had been waiting for her. Or waiting for someone. He looked up, straight up at the window, his head turning just too far to be natural. And finally he smiled.

And finally he was gone.

A HOUSE BUILT FOR TWO
TAMMY A. BRANOM

Gray winter clouds hung overhead as my husband and I drove up the long, curved driveway to meet Sondra. At the top, nestled amid magnolia bushes, hedgerows, and lines of trees, the quaint, one bedroom cottage peaked out.

Sondra, friend and caretaker of the estate, explained to me over the phone that the owner, Virginia, recently had been moved to a care facility for the elderly. Now, Sondra needed someone to move into the house and watch over it and the grounds until either Virginia returned to her home or she passed away.

Virginia's husband, Robert, had died many years ago. Childless, she had no one to visit her other than friends. Therefore, after Robert's demise, she had lived by herself in the house he had built for her in 1923. She spent her days alone in her residence sitting in her overstuffed chair staring at the television.

Once inside, we gathered in the living room. Sondra sat in Virginia's green chair. Looking around the room, she heaved a sigh and related to us the story of when she knew the time had come for Virginia to leave her beloved home holding all the precious memories of her and Robert together.

One afternoon, shortly after Sondra got off work, she drove to Virginia's to look in on the eighty-ish woman and take care of whatever needed done. Although Sondra kept a regular schedule, Virginia rarely remembered visits anymore. In fact, most days, Sondra found the small, frail lady sleeping in the living room.

That day was no different.

Virginia had fallen asleep again in her favorite place, her chair, with the television blaring. As Sondra clicked the TV off, Virginia opened her eyes and smiled.

"Robert?"

"Virginia," Sondra called out. "It's me."

Her lips still curved upward in a small smile, Virginia gazed to the empty leather chair next to hers and whispered into the air as if talking to someone. Sondra moved closer to hear the conversation, and Virginia suddenly looked up at her friend, her eyes wide with surprise.

"Sondra!" Virginia exclaimed. "When did you get here?"

With a deep sigh, Sondra clasped her friend's hand. "I just got here."

"I was telling Robert just now that it was almost time for you to come over."

"Virginia..." Sondra sighed again, shaking her head.

"Yes, dear?"

"You know Robert is gone."

"Gone?" Virginia glanced to the vacant recliner and back. "Oh no, dear. He's not gone. Here's right here in his chair."

Upon conclusion of her story, Sondra's forehead wrinkled and she hung her head. "That's when I knew she needed more care than I could give."

Little did I know "the devil was in the details" of her account.

Sondra showed us around. The house was still as cozy as when Robert and Virginia called it home. The small, one bedroom cottage style is perfect for a couple with no children, as we were as well. In later years, Robert constructed an extra room off the kitchen and dining room as a study for himself. In a corner of the basement, behind the furnace, Robert's workbench still stood with numerous tools and household fix-it items stashed in the cupboards and drawers and hanging on the wall on pegboard.

After the short tour, Sondra turned to us and asked, "So, what do you think? I know it needs a little fixing, but it's still a solid house. The wind won't blow it down."

With a quick look between us, my husband and I agreed this was the place for our two Chihuahuas and us.

"We'll take it," I said without hesitation. "It's perfect."

Just like that, my husband and I lucked into renting this cute little home. However, our luck was short lived. When we moved in, the house immediately began having problems, as if in retaliation to us being there.

Lights started dimming and flickering all over the household. Daily brownouts (they had nothing to do with the electric company) popped light bulbs in every room. Worried the erratic power surges would destroy the microwave, television, or any of the appliances, or worse yet, start a fire; I insisted an electrician come in. He couldn't find a problem; much less repair whatever was going on. All he could do was replace the old breakers, which he did.

Of course, that didn't change a thing. As unusual as I thought the occurrences were, my husband, being a former soldier, did not accept anything as "unexplain-able."

"It's just old wiring," rationalized my husband in his ever-logical way; his arms folded over his chest. Nothing disturbed him.

His argument was valid in my mind, but after the first week in the house, "perfect" was no longer the word, I would use to describe the cottage. We over-heard our names called out, but neither of us had said a word. I heard and felt footsteps traversing the main house floor and in the attic. Many times, I woke in the middle of the night to sounds of boxes dragging across the attic, as if someone was moving stuff around. When checked, there was no one or anything. No scuffmark were apparent, nor was dust disturbed any-where. Cold breezes gusted throughout the household at random intervals, but we never found a source.

And that was just the beginning. As time went on, more strange things happened, although my husband generally came up with justifications to discount most of them. Shadows fluttered over the walls, even at night. A strong odor of a woman's perfume would oc-casionally drift in the vicinity of Virginia's chair (we were using it for a while) and dissipate as swiftly as it came. Sometimes there were knocks on the door, but no one was around. The dogs would not enter the add-on den. They stood at the doorway and craned their necks to peer inside, only to turn and run away. That room always stayed very cold, no matter the season or the house temperature.

Then there was the basement.

Shortly after we moved in, a severe thunderstorm barraged the area along with several days of torrential rain, flooding creeks and swelling rivers beyond their banks. In the middle of the final tempestuous night, non-stop brilliant lightning shards blazed the sky. It was as if the heavens opened up and the universe poured down on our little corner of the world. The basement took on water, seeping through the walls and bubbling up from the floor.

One blinding bolt lit up the backyard, and the electricity went out. We thought lightning struck the tree behind the house.

The next morning, when power crackled again in the lines of our neighborhood, everyone had electricity except us in the cottage. Apparently, something shorted somewhere, but we could not find the problem. From our windows, we saw the electric box lying on the ground, dangling from the pole by the heavy line attached to it. We called an electrician, but because of the storm, it would be hours, maybe even days, before he could get there.

We needed to get the water out of the basement. An electrician would never work in the artificial pond downstairs, so I became committed to forcing out the flood. I waded barefooted into the freezing, knee-high water to open the cellar door to the backyard. Water rushed the exit like a raging mob.

Using a snow shovel, I pushed the remaining inches of the lagoon out bit by bit until, after an hour, it receded to my ankles. A stick floated by me on its way out with the remainder of the pond. Being too big to make it out of the doorway, I stopped shoveling, reached into the water, and picked it up. A tingling sensation ran up my arm. I stood up with a jerk. It wasn't a shock that could knock me unconscious; merely a slow prickling through my muscles and skin.

I called to my husband and he rushed down the stairs to me.

"Watch this," I said as I plunged my hand in the water again. "I'm getting shocked from the water, but only when I touch it with my hand. I'm not being shocked anywhere else."

We stared at each other. The power was not on yet. There was no electricity for me to get shocked.

"Get out of the water," he ordered, moving up the stairs. "Don't touch anything; just get out." I shrugged and did as he said. On the way out, I leaned on the dryer, which wasn't in water, but I still was in to my ankles. As I laid my hand on the metal, I had a shock delivered to me making me see stars. I guess I should have paid more attention to my husband when he said not to touch anything. Lesson learned.

Hours later, the electrician finally showed up, came in, and examined everything. The conditions he found perplexed him. He also discovered the electric box hanging from its pole, but the meter inside was gone. He searched nearby, but it was nowhere in the vicinity. When he came to us to us to explain the situation as best he could, he started by saying he had never seen anything like this before. At first, he thought we were using some other method to get power, but when the main office verified we were indeed paying for our electricity, the circumstances became more curious. It was an educated presumption on his part, but he didn't think lightning had struck the pole or the tree.

He presented another explanation.

A neutral line had separated from the main power line connecting from the street to the meter in the backyard. The neutral line touched the saturated ground and electrified the water in the backyard and into the basement. However, he could not explain the missing meter. Strangely, he said it appeared as though someone ripped the box from the pole with a crowbar and removed the meter, leaving the lock intact and uncut, which was impossible.

He (and other electricians he collaborated with) were dumbfounded I was not electrocuted the second I stepped into the water. Some said it wasn't until I made the electrical loop with my hand in the water that I was in danger. Some even joked I had a guardian angel that day.

I didn't think it was an angel, but perhaps someone else who did not like the water in the cellar. Oddly, the only section of the cellar untouched by water was Robert's workbench. This was "his" area and no one else's, like many men who have such a cubbyhole in their home or garage. Although the entire basement was flooded, that corner, behind the furnace, remained dry.

I began to wonder if perhaps my husband and I were not wanted in the house. The possibility occurred to me that Robert and Virginia didn't like us using their possessions. As a young couple, we didn't have a lot of furniture of our own, so my husband suggested making use of the furnishings for ourselves, such as a vanity, dressers, the dining table, and several cabinets, along with dishes and some pots and pans. In addition, we utilized all of the living room furniture, including Virginia and Robert's sofa, accessory tables, and their old chairs as well as.

One day, I took a good, hard look at the furnishings and decided to "clean house," so to speak.

"Those definitely need to go," I said, pointing to Virginia's green overstuffed chair and Robert's leather recliner. "They're ugly and have an odd smell, too."

My husband vehemently agreed. Without any hesitation, he opened the doors, dragged the chairs into the backyard, broke them up, and burned them in the fire pit.

I hoped things would quiet down if their chairs were gone.

As I continued my clean up, I rummaged through drawers full of the elderly couple's belongings, and I found a picture of Robert and Virginia along with several other photos.

The grainy black and white prints showed diminutive Virginia as a young girl propped casually against a car dressed in the fashion of the '20's or '30's; her hair barely longer than the hat snuggling her head. Robert towered next to her, a lean, square-faced handsome man. His attire also spoke of simpler times with a white button-down shirt and light pants.

The picture made me smile for them. They appeared happy in the snapshot, young and in love. The best part of it was, at least I now knew what they looked like. I had faces to put with the names and with the house. I put the photo back with the others in the same place I found them, not that I thought moving them would be disturbing Virginia or Robert, but so I would remember where they were later.

After the cleanup, the shuffling noises escalated and lights blinked when no television or appliance was running. The incidents happened so often; we tried blocking them out, ignoring them. We went so far as to make more excuses as to why things were still going on, but we never truly grew accustomed to them. I wondered if the disposal of the chairs had anything to do with it.

The old house creaked and groaned, as to be expected. And, as is common with aging homes, cold spots seeped in. However, drafts in the house were more like light winds. As the winter months stretched on and the days and nights plummeted to freezing temperatures, we sought out the unexplained breezes in an effort to seal out the cold. Nonetheless, one night an icy draft blew through the living room as if all the windows were open. It pushed into the room with determination, along with heavy footsteps plodding from one end of the house to the other and straight past me to where the leather chair once sat.

My hair rustled from the gust and my skin prickled. The newspaper I left on the end table fluttered to the floor. To me, that was a sign. Robert missed his chair.

Then came something new to taunt our senses.

Perfume. Not a nice, soft scent, but the "ode de toilet" aroma that burns your nose, tears your eyes, and reminds anyone of their great-grandmother. The noxious odor hovered for several minutes at a time where Virginia's green chair formerly sat. Moreover, if the television happened to be on when the scent formed, the perfume lingered longer than usual, and the channels changed of their own volition. Eventually, after a long, random channel search, the power strip popped and shut off the TV. The problem was not with the remote control. It was brand new with fresh, top quality batteries. It was not the television, either. We purchased it only a few months prior to moving into the house. Nothing made sense. Sometimes even a new breaker flipped off as well. As the TV channels continued to flick to different programs by themselves, I could only conclude that Virginia evidently couldn't decide what to watch.

The perfume scent was just as problematic. My husband rented a rug scrubber and cleaned the carpets, especially around the area where Virginia's chair had stood, since that's where the odor conglomerated when it manifested. Nevertheless, the perfume still returned at erratic intervals. Undeterred, he, of course, found a logical explanation.

"She sat in the same place for so long, the smell permeated the carpet and floor underneath," he stated.

Although he had a solid solution, I still felt something else was going on there. However, since Virginia was not dead, I couldn't grasp that SHE was haunting the home. Robert, yes, but it was Virginia's perfume wafting around HER chair. Resolute to figure it out, I read several books on spirit manifestation and visitation that was not connected to the dead. After a couple weeks of research, my conclusion, albeit confusing and complicated, made sense when considered with the understanding that the human brain is not yet entirely understood and can seemingly do things on its own, separate from our conscious minds. The basic idea is that a deep desire to have something, be somewhere, be someone else, or even have a "friend" (as in an "imaginary friend"), can be fabricated by the subconscious psyche. So, what I deduced is that in the same way stressed youth can create poltergeists, perhaps the Alzheimer's disease allowed the elderly woman the freedom of mind to continue living in the house. And, if one believes in an afterlife along with ghosts and spirits capable to walk among us after death, she may have been able to see Robert and spend time with him again in a subconscious realm generated by her yearning to be home with him. She literally was in the house with Robert. On the other hand, maybe she just wanted to be home and not in a care facility. Nonetheless, the perfume was hers. I found a bottle of it in the bedroom. There was no mistaking the overbearing scent.

Not only my husband, the dogs, and I noticed the strangeness in the house. My daughter and her husband came to visit for a week. I set up the hide-a-bed sofa in the living room so they could stay with us instead of shelling out the money for a hotel room. After the first night, they complained of a draft they spent most of the night trying to locate. Several times, they thought they succeeded, but as they settled down to sleep again, the breeze returned. It became so cold; the heavy comforters I gave them didn't keep them warm. Then, to top it off, the rank perfume hung in the air for almost an hour. Needless to mention, they did not get any worthwhile rest that night. But, for the remainder of the week they stayed, there were no other occurrences during the night.

While there, I gave my daughter a full tour of the house, showing her little details of the aged residence and obviously antique items left in the home. All went fine until we entered the basement. We walked around and I pointed out to her some deteriorating blocks of the foundation, in particular the one in which Robert etched their names and the year he built the house. I also wanted her to see the old tools of Robert's still hanging on the wall, so I motioned her to follow me and we went behind the furnace to the wooden work-bench.

"It's creepy over here," she said, and slowly backed away. She rubbed the chill from her arms and refused to stay down there any longer. She turned and headed up the stairs. Once we were in the safety of the main house, we sat down at the dining room table, and she told me the back corner, by Robert's workbench, was inordinately fearsome to her. She explained it was like a big cold spot and shivers rushed over her entire body. She also claimed she saw a shadow resembling a person, a tall man, peeking from behind the furnace, directly across from the workbench.

I was astounded. I had told her about a presence in the house, specifically in the living room and most like-ly in the den, but I had said nothing of the basement. She was surprised as well. Neither of us expected any-thing strange to happen while in the cellar, so for her to have a specific reaction and see a form gave me more evidence of at least one presence in the home.

Confirmation was all around me, perhaps even coming from the outside as well.

One morning, I was jolted awake to booming knocks on the front door. The dogs burst from a dead sleep also and ran to the door, jumping around and barking in their dance-like greeting. Groggy, I stum-bled out to answer the banging.

No one was there.

Since the dogs had responded to the noise, I knew it wasn't my imagination. Naturally, I checked the door to verify the wind was not the culprit. Although old, the door fit snug in the frame. In fact, scrapes of tattered wood splintered a scar into the threshold from the door dragging for years. I tested every conceivable notion I had and determined neither wind nor hand rattling could make or even imitate the rapping sounds. However, the heavy knocking persisted, mostly early in the morning, although sometimes in the afternoon when I would be in the kitchen, the thumps shook the door violently. I often turned to see the door actually moving in conjunction with the bangs, shaking in the frame, and there was no wind or anyone outside to create the effect. Was someone trying to come in or go out? I never could figure that out, but the knocks kept on. And, the ever-vigilant dogs charged the door every single time, announcing the intrusion with their boisterous yaps.

The dogs were always keen to the quirks in the home. There was one room, though, the dogs refused to enter.

The den.

In the 1970's, Robert built an extra room off the dining room and kitchen as a study for himself. Windows walled the room and his stacked books columned the underneath of the sills. A roll top desk filled one corner. Like his workbench, this was Robert's personal space.

At no time would either dog cross the den door's perimeter. They hunkered in the doorway and stretched their necks to peer inside, only to duck down and scamper away as if someone tried to pet them and they didn't like it. I didn't stay very long in there myself. Neither did my husband. The room always stayed icy cold, even in 100-degree days in summer. Our lone air conditioner was on the other side of the house in the bedroom, and it was so small it scarcely cooled the bedroom, much less any other part of the cottage. In the beginning, nothing bizarre happened inside the room, but that soon changed.

Preparing dinner one evening, I caught a glimpse of a man darting into the den. While brief, I observed enough of the figure to notice his height and his white shirt and light pants. The dogs followed him, stopping outside the door into the room. They sat there, staring in, wagging their tails and peering up at someone.

Although the clothes were nothing I recognized of my husband's, I believed it was him toying with me.

"I saw you," I yelled. "Besides, the dogs are giving you away." I tiptoed to the den and leaned through the doorway, hoping to sneak up on my husband and maybe give him a startle.

No one was in there.

"Whom are you talking to?" my husband said from the living room behind me.

My heart jumped two inches in my chest and my jaw almost bounced off the floor. I marched to the living room and confronted my husband. "That wasn't you?"

His face scrunched. "What are you talking about?"

"I saw you go into the den."

He shook his head no. "I don't know who you saw, but it wasn't me. I've been sitting here watching TV."

"I swear it was you."

Throwing up his hands, he turned his attention back to the television show I had interrupted. "I'm telling you, it wasn't me."

"I know I saw a man go in there. If it wasn't you, then…" My voice trailed off and I ran back to the den and stood inside, replaying the figure in my mind. I knew those clothes. I knew that man.

Frantic, I tore everything from the drawer until I found the photo again. The man in the picture matched the man I glimpsed in the den.

It was unmistakably Robert and in the same clothes as in the picture.

I needed no further convincing the cottage was haunted. It seemed he was just as curious about me as I was about him. He simply was "invisible" when checking into me.

Finally, after six months, and vexed by the goings-on, I sat down at the dining room table, prepared to confront Robert and explain how it was going to be around the house.

"We are not leaving," I announced into the air. "But, I won't ask you, too, either." I waited, expecting something to happen. Maybe a whisper. Anything.

"We're going to have to live together," I stated firmly. Nothing happened. But, nothing changed, and nothing worsened. Slowly, I became accustomed to the oddities, and we all simply resided in the humble abode.

Three years passed.

Instead of knocks one morning, I heard the front door close. Not a slam, merely a closing as if someone was leaving. Later in the day, Sondra called with the news Virginia had passed away. From that moment forward, there were no more whiffs of perfume, the footsteps and breezes ceased, and only the typical creaks and knocks of an old house carried on. In addition, the lights stopped flickering. The channels stayed put on the television. The den remained cooler than the rest of the house, but not the bone-chilling cold it was before. The dogs actually began sleeping in there.

And, I never saw Robert again.

I like to think Robert stayed in the house to look after his wife and their home until she departed this world to be with him in his. When that finally happened, Virginia and Robert left their house he built just for the two of them -- for one last time.

KNOCK, KNOCK
PAUL S HUGGINS

As I trawled through the loft I came across the boxes of books, photos and documents left with me by my grandfather. As I picked through them to find the animal encyclopedias my daughter needed for her homework, something dropped out from between them. Putting the pile of books on a joist and using the dull light of my torch I fished the little book from the glass fiber insulation. It glinted as the gold leaf embossed text caught the light. Intrigued I popped it into my trouser pocket, I grabbed the tomes I was up there to fetch and manhandled myself back through the loft hatch and lowered myself down to the waiting step ladder.

As I reached the dining room I placed the animal books in front of my daughter as she scribbled away at her homework on the dining room table. She briefly looked up and thanked me with a smile. I continued into the living room where I took a seat on the couch. Shifting over slightly I fished the small book from my pocket.

It was a diary from nineteen eighty four. I thought back to that time, I was fifteen and preparing to leave school. It seemed like an age away. I opened it, my maternal Grandfather's name and details were diligently added in the appropriate spaces on the inside cover. I reminisced about that great man whom I loved dearly in life, and passed away the year after this diary was used.

I looked through the first few pages. It was normal run of the mill stuff. He had been quite fastidious, much like myself, when dealing with appointments and keeping notes. Every Thursday appeared to be pension day, where he made the long walk to the Post Office to collect his meager hand-out. Every month his visit to the doctor was listed, Granddad suffered from angina and diabetes and depended on the doctor for the treatment of both.

Despite the two serious health problems for a Seventy four year old he was still incredibly active and spritely, which made his death a sudden shock at the time. He was also very creative and artistic, for which I am pleased to have inherited that trait. My Grandmother, Florrie, had passed away many years before in nineteen seventy three of cancer. According to his diary granddad still remembered her every year with her birthday and their wedding anniversary still added in to the appropriate dates. He had loved her very much but had settled into the life of a widower very well. He fended and looked after himself without help.

It was nice to get an insight into his everyday life, as opposed to just visiting him every couple weeks on a Sunday for dinner and the inevitable large chocolate bar to take home. As I flicked through I felt elated that this small journal with entries written nearly thirty years earlier was bringing back to me a flood of happy childhood memories.

As I neared the end of the diary heading towards the Christmas period of that year an entry had me perplexed. It didn't really fit in with previous notes.

Wednesday December 12. 1am there was loud knocking on the front door, I answered but no-one was there.

How very odd that Granddad should mention

someone doing the old knock and run, banging on doors then hiding as the householder swore at the inconvenience. I continued flicking through the pages, and then I came across another.

Thursday December 27. Heavier knocking on front door at 1am only stopped a couple of seconds before I answered it. No-one could be seen in the street when I opened the door.

That was it for nineteen eighty four. I needed to find the next diary, I was pretty certain there were more of these strange entries. So back up the step ladder I went. I found the box with all the old family photos that came from his. I was certain there was a rolled up carrier bag containing odds and ends such as maps, flyers and above all other diaries. Perched on the edge of the loft hatch I removed a couple of old photo albums from the top and fished around in the loose photos. In the fading light of the dying rechargeable torch I finally made contact with old and brittle plastic bag.

I pulled the bag free and while resting it in front of the box, I replaced the albums back in position. I lowered myself through the hatch and descended the ladder. I sat on the top step of the staircase. The bag was old and sported the logo of some long defunct company.

I pulled a few of the larger items from the bag to get down to the smaller items at the bottom. First out was nineteen eighty two. Thankfully there weren't many and the second one was my holy grail, Nineteen eighty five, the year he passed away. It wasn't dissimilar to the previous year's diary different typeface but still gold leafed.

It didn't take long to find another one of these entries.

Friday January 4. Tonight I was woken by someone calling my name, and the knocking on the door started again. I got downstairs as fast as I could, still no-one there.

The occurrence was happening a bit more regularly now.

Tuesday January 15. Florrie called for me tonight; I clearly heard her voice before the knocking started. It stopped as I opened the door.

There seemed to be a lot more hope in my granddads writing now, maybe he believed Grandma was trying to tell him something. Then I found an entry which referred to the last time I saw him.

Sunday February 3. My daughter visited today which was nice; I couldn't tell her what I wanted to, I did have a moment with her husband who was concerned but he think someone is probably just playing tricks on me.

That's my dad all-over, always the realist. The next one felt like granddad was becoming quite drained from it all.

Friday February 8. I now have trouble falling asleep, and it's no longer a surprise when the knocking starts, like tonight.

Monday February 11. She called to me again, when I got to the door as always nobody there, I miss her so much.

Tuesday February 12. Tonight I waited up. She called to me, it was Florence. I opened the door as the knocking started. There was nobody but a cloud of ether vanishing before my eyes. I am so very tired.

That was the last entry in the diary, the rest of the

book was empty with pristine pages kept mint by its brethren. Granddad passed away on Valentine's Day, February 14, 1985. I was shocked that this man who was a part of me seemed to sense his time was near and managed to convey it to me in so few words.

I decided to contact my father to find out what he knew about my grandfather's death as he had a mention in one of the entries, it would have been just too distressing for my mum, being her father.

The phone rang a few times until the familiar sound of my father's voice answered.

"Hello." He said

"Hi Dad" I greeted

"Oh hello son, how are you?" he said sounding happy to hear from me.

"Yeah good, Look Dad, I was wondering if you knew much about Granddads death." Dad wasn't much for small talk so I got straight to the point.

"Blimey that was thirty years ago." He said sounding surprised.

"I found some of his old diaries with some books and photos in the loft. There were some strange entries about Grandma visiting him just before he died."

"Oh yes I knew all about that, he was convinced. Listen son, don't tell your mother, but when I saw him about a week or so before he died, he took me aside because he wanted to confide in me. He told me that your grandmother had been calling on him."

I said "Yes it was in his diaries. Was he, you know, going a little crazy by the end?"

"Oh no not at all, he was right as rain as always. I remember your Uncle wasn't very happy with the emergency response. Apparently the police had registered an emergency call in the early hours on the night he died, because they couldn't understand his breathless speech they didn't send a copper round till about breakfast time. At which time they found he'd died in his chair in the living room of heart failure hours earlier" he explained.

"About the same time he was having the visitors in the night." I reasoned

"I suppose so. Mind you the last part he told me might fit."

"What was that?" I queried.

"He was quite convinced that your grandmother was warning him his time was near, he knew in his own mind if he opened the door and she was there, his time would be up and he'd get to be with her again."

After ending the call with a promise of taking the family round for lunch on Sunday I sat back. I was feeling quite content, although my father probably still believed it was youths messing about, I didn't. I felt quite safe in the knowledge that my Grandfather and Grandmother are together again.

THE DARK MAN
MELINDA DERFLER

Where does one begin writing just one ghost story, when their whole childhood was filled with experiences? I guess my story begins in the early 70s, when I was a young girl, the youngest of four children, growing up in a small house, full of entertainment, music and the occasional party. Not to mention teenage sibling squabbles, three females reaching puberty within a four-year time span and basically being raised by nannies, while my parents were out playing "club dates." My mother was a singer and my father was a guitar player/composer, as well as a piano tuner during the day. I think this lack of parental presence added to our desire and our freedom to experiment with the paranormal: Holding séances, using Ouija boards, reading Tarot cards and casting spells, were as commonplace to me and my siblings as playing Monopoly would be to other, more cautious children. However, frankly, for all that dabbling, and the lure of fighting pubescent children, surprisingly nothing ever really came out of it.

That is, until one night when everything changed.

At the time, my brother had a good friend, Tony, whose family had a spirit living with them most of his life. The spirit's name was April. Everywhere that Tony went, April was sure to follow.

Now as I understand it, April was pretty much a mischievous spirit, wreaking havoc upon Tony's family at any given time. Banging away on his brother's drum set to the point where they had to actually dismantle it! She seemed to be present quite often around Tony, uncannily attracted to him and perhaps keeping him safe from entities that may otherwise try to do him harm. I mention April only to point out the fact that my brother's friend was living with and comfortable with the presence of spirits. The obvious conclusion would be to hold séances to show others that the spirits he lived with every day were real. The problem with attracting spirits, however innocent the reason is that once you've gotten their attention, there is no way they can be controlled. And it's even harder to make them go back to wherever place they came from in the first place. No rescinding THAT invitation!

One night, my brother, Tony and his friends were down in my mother's basement holding a séance, while my sisters and I were upstairs. All of a sudden, we hear a loud whooshing noise, like an immense vacuum sucked the air out of the house, then screams and everyone came running upstairs, white-faced and out the door they went. After all these years, I was finally able to find out from my brother what happened, as until now, he would never speak of it. Evidently, some of his female friends decided to sit around a wooden table to hold a séance, while the guys watched. With their hands on the table, fingers touching, they began. All of a sudden, their hands started to rise up off the table! When they tried to push their hands back down on the table, they could not, as some strong invisible force was stopping them from doing so, pushing up as hard as they were pushing down. Then, everything happened at once. The girls screamed and jumped up, the table fell or "flew" as my brother put it, the chairs fell backwards (all this creating the bang) and up the stairs they ran, out the door never looking back. I bet they even left their purses, jackets and everything else behind, leaving my brother and Tony to literally pick up the pieces.

My theory is the "whoosh" that we heard was the portal opening up, perhaps something they could not hear downstairs due to all the commotion going on post-séance. From that moment on, until the end of the 90s, there was a dark entity now living in my mother's house. It's as though, through this last séance, they finally and successfully punched a hole into another dimension, allowing a malevolent spirit to enter. Heck, the entity was probably sitting there buffing his nails anticipating the opportunity when the veil between our world and his was at its thinnest and shoved his way merrily in. With the number of séances we were all holding, chipping away at that veil, it really was only a matter of time before one of us successfully punctured the membrane. The Dark Man, as my nephew officially dubbed him, had arrived and our idea of the paranormal was about to change.

That night, The Dark Man decided to choose his first victim. He chose my mother. She heard her name being called in my father's voice, in the "dead of night," which is what woke her up. She reached over and felt that my father was sound asleep. All of a sudden, something grabs her by the shoulder and starts violently shaking her back and forth, as she lay on the bed! She turns on the light, the shaking stops, but when she looks at the closet door, it is sliding open and shut at an inhuman rate of speed, WITH NO SOUND AT ALL! The movement was way too fast for any children to be doing it, not to mention it was 3:00 in the morning. Uncanny I think is the word here. The next day, she had bruises on her arm that looked as though left by someone grabbing her and, well, violently shaking her. First thing she did was go to my brother and say, "Whatever you have been doing down there, you need to stop doing it!" And he did. But mom didn't tell her daughters to stop. Oh no. We were her little innocent daughters that she dressed up all alike and paraded around like little angels at Easter. Blame the son instead. She never said anything directly to us, so we were free and clear! My brother may have stopped holding séances in our basement, gallantly taking the blame for what we were all doing. But my sisters and I continued, despite our mother's request to the contrary. We just didn't tell her what we were up to. After all, she was out working at night. And now that she told our brother not to do it, we were entering the Forbidden Fruit arena, thus escalating the adrenalin rush of doing something we KNEW we'd be punished for if we got caught. We still kept frigging around with séances, Ouija, Tarot and spell casting, like stupid little witches, dabbling with the occult. "Bubble, bubble, toil and trouble." Indeed, a VERY stupid, or should I say ignorant, thing to do. No, swap that. I do mean stupid.

But the séances no longer really mattered. The Portal was open now. Whatever came through at any given time had free reign. Who knows? Maybe The Dark Man was a kind of Pied Piper tooting his little Spook Horn, calling one and all to come on in, have a good time terrorizing this unsuspecting family! He sure seemed to be the Leader of the Band, the darkest, most corrupt and evil of them all. Perhaps he ruled the basement with an iron fist, keeping the weaker spirits under his domain and making them do his bidding.

And there were others who came; lesser beings that would make their presence known, but they didn't seem harmful; more playful than anything; touching your hair, whispering in your ear. Taking things that you know were there just a moment before, then finding them days later at the most ridiculous spots; on top of the refrigerator, behind the piano. Like a framed photograph from one bedroom in someone else's dresser drawer under their clothing. Irritating things like that. But it was obvious that a door had been opened and basically anyone passing by who wanted to come in to a house full of pubescent children and feed off their energy and fears was doing so. And they were apparently enjoying the hell out of the opportunity.

A little later in the 70s, my brother having come home from Vietnam, started going out with a Greek girl named Connie, whose own home was quite actively haunted. So much, so that they had an Ouija board they left on a coffee table all the time. It would move of its own accord, conveying some random Information of the Day, such as "3WM, 3WM" over and over. Three weeks after this occurrence, their Uncle Mathew died. Connie's mother, who was full-blooded Greek and married to a full-blooded Native American man (both powerful nationalities), practiced black magic and welcomed spirits openly. I had my own experience there, while babysitting Connie's little girl in the late 70s, which I'll tell about a little later in this story.

Our whole childhood was spent being afraid of The Dark Man in the basement, what it would do to us next or what we would see. The Dark Man was especially active when one was alone or at night. Growling, scratching your back as you went up the basement stairs, tripping you as you went downstairs, watching you always from the dark side of the basement, following you around down there until you got the hell out. Shutting off each lifeline of light as you left, then making that last brave turn towards the stairs. And you couldn't get up the stairs fast enough. It's as though one was being pushed. And if you weren't fast enough, that's when you got scratched. They sure as hell enjoyed the Fear Factor Shot they produced from your sorry ass each and every time…for them it was probably like doing a shot of tequila. You knew something was right behind you every single time you walked up those basement stairs. I couldn't have turned around to look if my life depended on it. Nope. Just get down and back up as quickly as possible. Or take the coward's path through the garage. For some reason, those four icky concrete stairs going into the basement from the garage had no spirit guards lurking about waiting indignantly for some stupid human soul to come blundering in. One could slip in, load some laundry and slip back out undetected. Or at least have the door slammed fast enough before they came zipping in from the main area. Ha! Fooled you again, You Creepy Freaks! Truly, they owned that basement and let everyone know it!

We'd see faces in mirrors or looking through the window at you. Lurking along the balcony outside, leaving no foot prints in the snow or just standing there staring at you from the closet. Black masses floating in front of a room full of people, knocking, banging and footsteps. Oh, always the damned foot-steps.

As I grew older, my brother and older sister moved out, leaving the large "girl's room" above the garage to me, and my other sister moved into my brother's old room on the main floor. Now having the large "girl's room" to myself was all fine and dandy, and I loved the extra space, with my own bathroom, a large double-door closet and a lovely wrap-around balcony that you could sneak off of at night to meet up with teen friends. But the room didn't have a door on it. Never did. Oh for sure it once had this vinyl accordion-like contrap-tion that one could struggle to close ALMOST all the way and it used a magnet to "lock" it. That stupid con-traption never did quite close all the way. There was usually a 2-3" black slit (of course), a dark black ma-levolent slit. You just KNEW damned well when you felt that something was right there peeking through that evil slit, they probably were. And sometimes, it seemed the slit got wider or narrower, even as one watched it…in the "dead of night" and no sound to ac-company the phenomenon. Nope. To me that never counted as a door, since it didn't close all the way for privacy at the very least or lock to give me even the tiniest bit of comfort as I dressed or slept or played up there. It was just another Dark Man Terror Tool to use against me.

No wonder my sisters couldn't wait to be next in line for "Kurt's Room." It had a blessed door on it! One that we believed would magically block out the stink-ing Dark Man.

Oh, and I have to mention something here. My mother had decided it would be cute to decorate our bedroom with clowns. CLOWNS! Clown head boards, clown pictures that watched your every move, clown posters, stuffed clowns, even a clown bas-relief staring down at you from over the bathroom, sticking out nicely so you could see him from all sides. Lord have mercy on my soul. There isn't a child out there who isn't in some way terrified of clowns. And this was way before the movie Poltergeist, with its demonic clown doll that the mother decided would look real nice sitting in a little chair facing the kid's bed. And we know what happened in THAT movie, right? But I digress...Once my sisters were out of the room, I took down the cursed clowns and opted for black-light posters of Jimmy Hendrix, Deep Purple and an overly-muscled naked woman on a Pegasus...for variety.

My nice big airy room, with its wrap-around balcony, very own bathroom, and super large closet just for me, was located STRAIGHT ahead of the basement door. You could flip a marble from the top of my bedroom stairs and it would roll all the way down into the dark, dank basement and plunk against the bar. Wouldn't surprise me at all if the Brave Little Marble would have started moving slowly to the left towards the side where the spirit hole was so obviously lurking, like a big giant marble-gobbling magnet...again, like the pull of the closet in Poltergeist. Wisely, we never actually tried this experiment, probably too afraid to wake up good old Dark Man with our little marble. Best to let him rest. After all, he was always having a busy night.

That was my first realization that anything really, really good usually comes with a hidden downside. My bright big All-To-Myself bedroom had a direct route

THE DARK MAN

to hell and it was coming for me almost every night. But at least I had the room to myself now.

Oh wait...that means I'm alone now. No sister to kick awake so she can experience the same mind-numbing terror that I was. No, she was now down in a nice toasty little bedroom with a magical door on it, while I was left behind in the wide open, Come and Get Me bedroom...the only room in the whole damned house that didn't have a door on it. Just a vinyl contraption that wouldn't close all the way.

So, most nights, late at night...you know, in the "dead of night"...there I'd be, sound asleep, when something would wake me up. A noise or maybe it was just that the air would get thick and cold. Your ears perk up, your skin gets goose bumps, even though you are buried under the covers, and your body tenses in fear. And it would start. Softly at first, barely audible...boom, boom, boom...the sound slowly and methodically growing louder as it moved closer. The sound of someone or some THING coming, coming, ups the basement stairs: Someone with 100-lb. steel-toed gob-stomping boots on, the sound echoing throughout the house. All your attention is on each step, counting the 14 basement stairs, knowing, JUST KNOWING, it knew you were awake and waiting in fear for what it would do next! 12...13...then it would reach the top of the stairs! 14! God, can't anybody else HEAR THIS? Or are they all listening to it as well, frozen in terror, counting the steps, too? Then you'd hear softer shuffling. Was it shuffling its feet on the tile floor, coming towards my stairs or down the hallway towards my family? Or worse, was it sniffing and snuffling, trying to scent who was awake? Should it come up for me or should it turn left and go for my sister, who had a nice thick magical door on her room? Then, the moment I'd hear the creak on the first step of my room, I'd freeze, paralyzed like a deer in a headlight, I'd stop breathing, start trembling and sweating, heart racing, body strung tight as a piano string, staring into the darkness of the stairwell, praying it wouldn't come any closer. Most times, it was as though it just stood at that first landing, watching me, and absorbing my fear. Sometimes I would see an intense blackness there, within the black of the stairway. I'd see the darkness detach and come racing towards me, or worse, slowly float towards me, just before I'd cover my head with the blanket and pass out from fear…if I was lucky. The worst times were when I saw it coming, covered my head and waited, picturing it's face just on the other side of the blanket, waiting for me to be just a tad brave enough to peek out. Was it still there or had it gone yet? Usually, I'd finally fall off to sleep, feeling the air getting lighter and warmer. Other times, after staring at the blackness for what seemed like an eternity, I'd relax. But it's as though it waited until I relaxed. Then, like the Shock Value Moment of a teen horror movie, it would strike. I'd turn over and it would be hovering above me, with its white face glowing. Scream and faint. Peek out from the covers and it would be there, in the bathroom, glowing like a monster: Scream and faint. One time, I turned over and a white hand comes up from under the bed and grabs my neck! Scream and faint. Thank heaven I would pathetically and instantly pass out from fear. Or maybe it was from holding my breath for so long. Either way, I was in the clear…at least until the next night.

Other times, it would simply slam the bathroom or closet doors. By the way, pulling the covers over the top of your head and shoving your fingers so far into your ears you can feel your brain does work. At least for me it did. Don't let anyone tell you differently. Out of sight, out of mind. I figured if I couldn't see it or hear it, then it had no power over me. This is probably why it would slam doors instead. Gotta get that terrifying last word in. Otherwise, stomping up the stairs wouldn't have been worth the extra energy and drama, right?

Of course, I had positioned my bed as far away from the stairs as one could possibly get, without it being on the outside balcony. But that didn't matter. What would 12 feet of distance matter when it could cross that distance in a heartbeat? I was at its mercy, with no one to scream for. They were on the other side of the house, probably hovering behind their nice magical bedroom doors, counting the steps, with the covers over their heads, hoping it went up the Come Get Me stairs instead of turning left.

It was a powerful entity, and it was having a gay old time. Sometimes you'd hear voices or someone call your name. It's scary knowing it knows all of our names, isn't it? One time, my sister was in the basement, which is finished beautifully, by the way, with lovely wood paneling and a bar in the center that my mother tiled. Pictures of people my parents worked with, and oil paintings my mother created. It was the perfect party spot to entertain all of their friends in the entertainment business. Not a bad environment for Good Old Dark Man to pull up a stool after a hard night's terrorizing and pour himself a Pibb No. 1.

It was also the place for us kids to hang out with friends or boyfriends and listen to the stereo. My mom had this interesting lounge chair that was shaped like an "S," with the back being the top curve and you could lay in it with your legs raised on the bottom curve. So, here's my sister, making out with her boyfriend (it was a great make-out sofa) and all of a sudden, she hears a male voice speaking right in her ear at the same time she sees an arm coming up from under the chair towards her. She shrieks and tells her boyfriend what she just saw; he tells her he just heard a female voice speaking in HIS ear, and thought it was her! What's really odd is that male and female voices were heard exactly at the same time saying the same words. Bet it was something like "Get Out," which always seems to be the catch phrase of the spirit world. Come on, guys. Get another line, would ya? But things like this became commonplace and almost expected. The classic haunting you hear about on TV. With a tad more terror sprinkled in for affect. For me, as a child, I felt that it was almost a normal thing, that everyone probably had their own spooks. Yet, it was a scary fearful childhood, filled with uncertainty.

Thinking of how this all started and why, I realize now that Connie, along with the open magic practicing of her very Greek mother, were also a huge influence on our holding séances, as well as accepting the consequences. We all did it. Not just my brother and his friends. That was the fun thing to do at our house! Especially since it almost always produced Amazing Results! But he and his friends got lucky, not to mention the fact that his close friend already had a foot in the door. They had the power to really truly reach the spiritual world.

Just going to Connie's house would convince someone that place just wasn't right. It always had a heavy atmosphere or cold spots. They had pictures of spirits in family photos. One in particular was amazing, where two family members, I think it was Connie's mother and father, were standing on the front walkway, right between the extremely tall privet hedges. Probably 10-feet tall they were. Next to the parents, on either side, were people standing, and they were AS TALL AS THE BUSHES! Tall slim pale transparent figures. You can't miss them in the picture.

In the late 70s, I was babysitting Jessica at Connie's Very Greek Spell-Producing Mother's house one day. It was a tri-level house. You walk in the front door: The kitchen is to the left, living room straight ahead, finished basement to the right down and bedrooms to the right up. I was playing with Jessica in the basement, while watching TV and came up into the kitchen to make us some lunch. I could watch her from the kitchen, as it had a direct view down. I look up to check on her, and she's standing up, staring at something that is left of the stairs, around the wall out of my line of sight...towards the washer/dryer room. She walks out of my line of sight and by the time I towel dry my hands to go see what mischief a 3-year-old is up to, I hear a deep snarl, like a wolf, a loud SLAP and Jessica comes running around the corner and up the stairs, SPLAT onto my legs like a leech. She is absolutely terrified and crying. When I kneel down to look at her face, she has a large red mark on her cheek, as though someone had slapped her!

Well, by this time, I'm about 16 or 17 years old, I've already taken karate lessons, worked in auto shop at school with a bunch of butt-grabbing guys, and beat up a few girls at the competing high school next town over. I was tough, could take care of myself, and I had a child to defend. Who the hell had gotten into that basement, was my obvious thought, figuring they hit the little girl who had discovered them while breaking in and going for the large TV and stereo equipment. It never occurred to me that it wasn't an intruder down there. And this was during a beautiful sunny day! So, I tell Jessica to sit on the kitchen floor where I can see her (and grab her to run out the front door if need be), I pull out one of Mr. Moore's Extremely Large Carving Knives and I slowly, but quietly go down the stairs. The further down I got, the colder it got. And I noticed a pungent, sour dead animal smell, which increased as I moved closer. I round the corner and as I'm getting closer to the washer/dryer room opening, my fear factor is increasing with each step, and the smell is making me gag. My arm hair is standing up and my instinct is telling me I am in extreme danger. I am just about to enter the room when I hear this very low and very deep growl...like a tiger. It was big, it was bad, it smelled like death and it was telling me it was going to attack if I came any closer.

I backed up, keeping my eyes on the doorway, until I was around the corner. Then, running up the stairs, swinging the knife behind me in case The Putrid Thing was chasing me, I throw the knife into the sink, grab Jessica and high-tail it out the front door (my escape route coming to me naturally, as I was planning it in detail in my head while I was inching closer to The

Stinking Rotting Thing In The Washer/Dryer Room).
I got into my car and drove around the corner, where I
had a clear view of the house from the side, front and
back doors visible, as well as the basement access door.

Tough indeed. I can handle any human being. But
an unknown growling stinking bestial someTHING?
Best to wisely retreat, dignity intact and wait for rein-
forcements.

I never saw anyone come out and I was able to
catch Connie when she came home. We crept into the
house, grabbed Mr. Moore's Extremely Large Carving
Knife and found nothing. No one. Not a thing. Zilch.

The house was back to normal temperature and the
smell was gone. And the basement door, which leads
outside, was bolted from the inside.

However, it was not long after this incident that I
heard that Connie's mother had vowed never to practice black magic again. Evidently, her mother had
woken up in the middle of the night and found an actual demon standing at the end of her bed! Large,
grey/green, muscular, bulbous, stinking and gro-
tesque. Oh lovely. Makes Good Old Dark Man look
like a schoolboy. Was this the monster that Jessica had
seen and been slapped by? Was this the fetid stinking
creature that growled at me from the darkened
washer/dryer room? Most probably, and I am ever
thankful that I listened to my instincts and got the hell
outta there. I don't know what it would have done to
me, but if it can physically slap a child, leaving a mark,
it could have done worse to me. Maybe with that big
old Mr. Moore Carving Knife I was carrying…burr. I
never went back to that house after hearing about the
demon. After all, I was used to ghosts. But demons?

That's a whole different threat level.

In the early 80s, I moved into my own apartment with my future husband, Jimmy, blessedly escaping The Dark Man's nightmare world. One night, we pulled up to my parent's house, as we were charged with watching the place while my folks were in California. All the lights were on, from the basement (you can see them through the glass block windows) to the Come Get Me bedroom above the garage. Thinking we had an intruder, my husband goes into stealthy Marine Corp mode (and he could be really stealthy...he was Native American). He checks all the windows, doesn't see anyone, so we plunge through the back door and BLINK! Every light goes off, instantly leaving us standing there dumb struck in an icy cold pitch-black house. You know how many lights there are in any given home? A lot. And it takes a lot of energy to do all that light switching. There was more than just The Dark Man in that house. Surely one entity couldn't turn off all those lights in one fell swoop? He must have had help. Or perhaps he did it all by himself (hence the extreme cold, a sign that all the energy is being absorbed in preparation for a manifestation). If so, I hope he pooped himself out big time that night. Thank God when that happened I had my non-believing husband with me. He was a believer from that day forward. Not to mention the fact that he was a Journeyman Wireman Electrician. He knew that if the house lights were all on, then all shut off at once, the street lights would also be off, due to loss of power on the outside lines. The only other excuse besides power loss to the grid is a LOT of people shutting the lights off simultaneously within the house. No, the situation was screaming paranormal and all of a sudden, his little Wife-E-Poo didn't appear as kooky about spooks as he had previously suspected.

I always wondered, after thinking of that night, how The Dark Man knew we were coming. Was he aware that we came to check on the house every day to bring in the mail and decide to spook us the next night? Or was he playing Let's See How Many Lights We Can Turn On and Off every night while my folks were gone? That's a more preferable thought than his consciously knowing my whereabouts at any given time. I do know that a couple days after this incident, Good Old Dark Man must have followed us back to our apartment. I caught his face reflecting in our fish tank one night, glowing in the darkened dining room. And the next night, I had a nightmare that I cannot recall. But when I woke up, I felt that same childhood terror. I lifted the blanket to turn from my right side to my left and when I did, his white evil face shot up from under the blankets towards my face, whoosh! Scream and faint.

Hey if that reaction protected me as a child and worked, I was sure as hell gonna use it as my go-to when I became an adult. At least at that time I did. The next day I told my husband what had happened. My parents were due to come home that evening. So he, being raised Catholic, decided we needed to head over there and bless the house. He dug out the tiny bible he was given at Communion, over to the house we go, pushing down our trepidations. We walked all over that house, arm in arm, saying the Lord's Prayer and reading passages from the bible. From the Come Get Me Bedroom all the way around the house and down into the basement, ending with standing in front of what one could feel was The Portal. It never showed up at our apartment again, perhaps realizing the little girl he enjoyed terrorizing had a mighty good, very strong pure-hearted man that was blessed by his church at her side and he was not to be messed with.

I can see The Dark Man's face to this day and can draw it very easily, burnt in my memory forever: His dark black sunken eyes looking out from white, white skin. He had high arched brows, long wide nose and wide mouth with white lips and dead man's teeth...a putrid mouth. Black slicked back hair, with sideburns. Side burns. When in time did he live to have those damned side burns, come to think of it?

There are many stories to tell of our childhood haunting. Too many to list here. But eventually, in the late 90s, my two sisters decided to work with my cousin to close the spirit doorway in my mother's basement. My cousin is a documented psychic medium and knew how to do the "canoe ritual," with success. After the ritual was performed, The Dark Man was gone and we no longer felt like we were being watched whenever we would go in the basement.

In October of 2009, a year after I had lost my beloved husband, I decided to take up paranormal research as something to do during the long winter. It was becoming really popular on television, and one could obtain all the necessary equipment over the Internet. Once I got my neat-o keen-o audio device, digital movie camera, EMF (electro-magnetic fluctuation) device and temperature gauge, I sat there wondering where I could go to test all my groovy equipment. Then I realized the obvious! I'll try it at my mother's basement!

Now by this time in my life, some 35-plus years later, I was looking back at my childhood experiences like anyone would: Did it really happen? Was it all in my head? Was it an over-active imagination brought on by my older siblings' behavior? I had talked myself into thinking it must have been in my head, because, as God is my witness, I really didn't expect to get any evidence in my mom's basement when I went over there with all my neat-o keen-o equipment! Especially since my sister's were adamant that the canoe ritual was a success. Knock yourself out, Min. That basement is clean.

Or so we thought.

So, over I go, actually with the intention of cleaning her basement (a good excuse to be down there as it was in sorry moldy mildew shape). I started by setting up a static (non-moving) audio device next to my EMF meter. I say aloud, "If there is anyone here who wishes to speak to me, talk into this little red light and I will hear you." I go out of the house to buy some cleaning supplies. When I return, I listen to the audio device and, much to my surprised delight I hear the EMF meter start beeping, then a man's voice say, "Deep Purple!" Class A EVP (electronic voice phenomenon) along with an EMF spike indicating an increase in electro-magnetism! JACKPOT!

Deep Purple, eh? What the hell does THAT mean? Actually, I went out, bought the Best of Deep Purple the next day, and played it full volume while I cleaned. After all, anyone specifically asking for Deep Purple from the spirit world must really want to hear it. With the volume as high as it would go, I was assured it would reach the other side, if not all the way to Jupiter. Maybe it was The Dark Man yelling through the membrane "Deep Purple" as a way of telling me it's him and he's recalling the poster from my bedroom. Who knows? But I was elated...absolutely floored to get the EVPs because it proved one very important thing to me: That all of my childhood experiences were NOT in my head. They DID happen to me. I had proof right there on my audio device that a spirit was speaking to me.

There are still residual spirits who are lurking about down there. Not the Big Bad Dark Man, but the quieter non-malevolent ones. Maybe they were there before The Séance and remained there after the spirit door was closed, somehow belonging on that property for whatever reason. I've gotten tons of movies of orbs coming out of the walls, lights moving about, and so many EVPs that there is no doubt they are there. They mimic what I say, such as the time I asked them to talk into the audio device, I'll be right back, I have to check my zucchini casserole in the oven. I get an EVP that says, "Zuc...Zucchini Casserole..." HA! Amazing.

Or what sounds like an Irish man singing, "Hey we like to, to say it, to say it, we like to. We absolutely like to....SAY IT!" in a sing song voice. At least he sounds like he's happy. What more could one ask for when stuck in my mother's basement for eternity?

I've stopped my research at my mother's knowing that if I continued I could very well re-invite something back in that shouldn't be there. Though I never evoked the spirits, simply asking them to come forth and speak is a way of inviting them. I didn't want them to get any stronger. Maybe my Good Old Reliable Instinct was telling me that The Dark Man was still there, on the other side of the thin veil, once again buffing his nails, patiently waiting for the next person to weaken the membrane so he can punch his way back in. Either way, there are many other places for me to take my neat-o keen-o equipment to, many other spirits waiting for someone to listen to their sad words. And I am no longer terrified of them. The more I try to understand them, the more I pity them. Pity has replaced terror.

To make sure my mother's basement was "quieted down," I did a Native American cleansing down there, abalone shell, sage smudge, wafted with a hawk feather while chanting the Sacred Prayer for Cleansing. It seemed to help, as orbs were no longer showing up in my snap shots. But they did show up in some pictures taken during a Halloween Party there in 2010, obviously enjoying the party and loving energy that was surrounding them, after so many years of silence down there.

One should never dabble in the paranormal or occult. If you are, one must educate themselves first and, most importantly, protect yourself spiritually. But with the lack of fear for spirits or ghosts, comes strength of character. I can sit in the dark in that basement now. They have no power over me. Perhaps that lack of fear comes from experiencing my husband's death. Certainly, that is the worst thing in life. So, what harm can a spirit do to me, simply by speaking to me, or making noise or showing itself? It is dead. I am alive and belong on this plane. But I am willing to listen to it, if it wants to say something into the equipment. Conquering my fears gave me power over something our instincts say shouldn't exist, but does. And frankly, most times you don't even know they are there until you look at the pictures or listen to the audio. Don't wanna see or hear 'em? Then don't turn on the equipment! Easy peazy.

At least one doesn't see things with the naked eye or hear most things with their own ears now that The Dark Man is gone.

Would I feel the same lack of fear if ever encountered The Dark Man again? Oh most assuredly. At least now, I react with angry strong energy as an instant response to fear. It's the old fight or flight instinct. Now that I'm an adult I can choose the fight instinct instead. That fight instinct also comes from the karate training, auto-boy butt-grabbing, girl-fighting youth I had. And I guess I'm a little pissed at the spirits for scaring me so much as a child. Especially the vindictive Dark Man. I'd love to be able to tell him to his face that he is nothing. A nobody. A lost pitiable soul who must have been a pathetic person in life, to be damned to walk the half-world tormenting young children in their sleep. Of course, that's assuming he ever had a human body, much less a soul in the first place, but I doubt he was any kind of demon. At least not like the horrifying one at The Moore House. Besides, there's still those damned side burns to think of...

Showing the spirits that I lack fear as an adult...well, I consider it a small token of revenge. I pity them. To be stuck in the spirit world forever, never moving into the light or what that light holds for us beyond. I can't think of a sadder thing to happen to the human soul. What did they do in life to deserve such a thing in death? Is that what Hell really is?

THE DARK MAN

What happened to me, as a child was real. I am thankful to my cousin and sisters for closing the spirit door successfully, thus eliminating The Dark Man from this world and saving future children from experiencing the nighttime horrors my childhood held. I am thankful to the spirits left there now, for communicating with me to let me know they exist. And letting me know I didn't imagine all of it.

There is but a thin membrane holding back The Other Side. A side that is full of the unknown, both malevolent and benevolent. Energies that are stuck there for eternity, just waiting for another chance to come back to this plane because they are incapable, for whatever reason, of moving onto the next plane: Salvation.

As one of my EVPs says, when I asked if they would wait for me while I ran upstairs, they replied, "We'll wait for you. We'll wait FOREVER!" I have no doubt in my mind that they will stick to their spine-chilling promise.

CHINESE TAKEAWAYS
JOHN IRVINE

Today is a cliché... clear, tropical blue sea with silver dust sparkling on its surface. Cloudless azure skies, golden syrup sunshine and a breeze just strong enough to fill the jib and main, both gulled out on poles. Our orange 40-foot plywood catamaran slides elegantly through the mirrored waters of Moreton Bay, and we four grown-ups loll about in the cockpit, all beautiful and bronzed, with cool drinks in fine glassware. The three small kids roll about squealing in the net strung between the bows; playing games, only they know the rules of.

It's the second to last day of our short holiday afloat, and we are determined to enjoy this last night "at sea." Our plan is to drop the pick in this quiet little bay on Stradbroke Island that we know of, make another jug or two of martinis, a pot of spag bog and enjoy the sun setting over the mainland, thankful that we aren't there.

We curl into the uninhabited cove, and Neil brings her up into the wind as I sheet in both sails. As he brings the bows up, I drop the jib to the deck, roll it up and secure it with elastic cords to the rail. The main is tied off to the boom, which I then tighten down with the boom vang.

Dot, Neil's wife, has dropped the big plough anchor, and the rattle of 100 feet of 3/8" short link galvanized chain clattering out through the pipe signals the end of the "working" day. Viv has the stove on fire in the galley, and the smell of onions drifts up through the forward hatch as I finish the foredeck tasks. I'm hungry now, and another of those vodka martinis wouldn't go astray.

The kids clamor for attention and food as I jump down from the side deck into the cockpit, hand out for my fresh drink. Viv does the honors. Now for that time-honored Queensland tradition, sundowners. As if we needed a reason...as Hoges says in the "throw-another-prawn-on-the-barby" ad in the US, "Beautiful yesterday, perfect today." Or something like that.

Eventually, the ankle-biters settle down, tummies filled with mince and spaghetti, and fall asleep below in their narrow pipe berths up in the bows. We chat quietly, watching the swirl of the outgoing tide in the channel between Stradbroke and the mainland, feeling content, and lulled by the almost imperceptible shiver of the boat in the swift tidal flow. Eyes begin to droop soon enough, and it's time to call it quits for today. Quiet goodnights are exchanged, and we collapse into our various bunks, tired but serenely happy.

* * *

I awoke with a start, and sit up, blinking in the moon-washed darkness. I listen, but hear only the water whooshing past the hulls, and feel a slight vibration through the cabin sole. Without thinking, I think *the tide's coming in*. A mental shrug and I decide that as long as I'm awake I might as well have a slash over the side. I'm uneasy, but push it away as I creep forward into the main saloon where Neil and Dot are sleeping. He's a rotten snorer, but I note that tonight, for once, he's silent.

It's about then that I see the gent standing at the bottom of the companionway down from the cockpit, backlit by moonshine. Not just any gent. Here we have a small wizened oriental fellow of indeterminate years, dressed in what looks to me like a Chinese mandarin's outfit, all gold fabric, quite long and complete with silver embroidered dragons. On his head is a small round pillbox hat like the missus used to wear to cocktail parties in the olden days. A long, grey plait hangs down his back.

Funny thing, although this was what one might call somewhat unusual I don't recall any fear or trepidation. I forget about the slash. Without taking my no doubt very wide eyes from Fu Manchu, I scrabble beside me for Neil's head.

"*Neil! Neil!*" I whisper this hoarsely, and, I think, rather loudly.

"*Whaaaaaa....*"

He sits up in his bunk while Dot sleeps on, and I take a quick glance at him. Neil's mouth looks like the entrance to the old Rimutuka train tunnel back home in NZ. "*Jesus!*"

My eyes flick back to our visitor, and he smiles at us, stretching out his arm and beckoning us with his hand, palm uppermost, fingers curling. His head with its very long, wispy silvery whiskers nods in perfect time to his gestures. Come, come... he seems to be inviting us to follow him. Neil slides from his bunk and the two of us shuffle forward like zombies as the Chinaman backs up the steep companionway steps with a smooth, gliding effect that is weirdly unnatural. As he exits backward through the open hatch he pauses, smiling and nodding again, and beckons more urgently. Then he just disappears. I blink, look at Neil, and then back up at the empty hatch. We bolt up on deck together in a rush.

As we exit the saloon, we automatically search the shore for markers. It takes a second, but Neil and I both realize at the same second that we're dragging the anchor. The strong incoming rip has dislodged the anchor somehow, and we're zooming backwards at an alarming rate. Fifty yards from the twin sterns we see the short reef which guards the southern headland, water creaming around the jagged coral and rock. What these razor-sharp buggers would do to our plywood hull doesn't bear thinking about. We are fortunate that tonight is an almost full moon in a clear sky, so our predicament is painfully obvious. We have maybe 10 minutes, max.

Neil leaps back into the cockpit and fires up the long leg outboard hanging between the hulls behind the cockpit. It coughs a couple of times, and then catches, and we surge ahead. I scramble forward to operate the winch as we motor up over the anchor, tramping my foot down hard on the deck switch. The rope hisses in, spraying warm sea water and phosphorescence everywhere, and then the welcome rattle of the chain indicates that the anchor almost up. Neil powers on as soon as he hears the chain, leaving me to make sure that the heavy anchor clears the side of the boat. We head out of the cove into Moreton Bay proper, and to safety.

During all this kerfuffle, the women and children sleep on, unaware. After a time Dot surfaces, puzzled sleepily about our middle-of-the-night departure. Neil suggests that she goes back to bed for now, and she does. We look at each other over mugs of hot coffee very liberally laced with Bundaberg rum, and grin.

Chinese takeaways will never be the same for us.

TUCKER'S COURT
DAVID PRICE

From the ages of ten to twenty-five, I lived in the house where my father grew up, which my grandfather bought in the nineteen twenties. Almost all of my childhood memories center on that house. It was the house where everyone liked to hang out. It was a fantastic neighborhood for kids, and I have great memories of the time spent with my friends there. Despite all the good times I had with family and friends in that house, it was a place where I was terrified to be alone.

We moved in with my grandparents when I was ten years old. Up until then, my family consisted of my parents, my younger brother, and myself. We had lived in few different two-family apartment buildings for the first ten years of my life. My grandparents still lived in their house on Tucker's Court, where they had been for over fifty years. We were always close to them, geographically and personally, so the transition was easy. We moved in with them because of their failing health. My grandmother, Lottie, had emphysema and needed to use an oxygen tank from time to time. She also had broken her hip and had to use a walker to help her get around. My grandfather, Babe, had suffered a heart attack several years before and had actually been legally dead for seven minutes. This caused him to have some memory problems, not severe, but enough that he could never get anyone's name right. He was more or less self-sufficient, but I think taking care of my grandmother was becoming too much for him alone.

I remember sitting in the living room with them, watching those goofy television shows that only grandparents watch. Lawrence Welk was my grandmother's favorite television show. I never understood why she liked it, but we all sat together and watched it. My grandfather loved Hee Haw. It was stupid, but at least I could appreciate the humor of it. There were others too. My grandparents weren't very mobile, so most of our entertainment was inside of the house. I remember watching those old seventies game shows like Match Game, The Newlywed Game, Family Feud, and, of course, The Price is Right. My grandmother was also fond of playing card games, so we would sit around the table playing rummy, crazy eights and any others she could teach me. My mother is a great cook, so she took over all the cooking duties. I think this was one of the most helpful things to my grandparents. My grandmother just couldn't do it anymore, and all my grandfather could cook was toast and tea.

I miss those times playing cards with my grandmother, even watching Lawrence Welk. When I was younger, she would play "This little piggy went to market," and "Peas porridge hot, peas porridge cold," with me. Living with them, even for just a little while, brought us all closer than we had ever been before. I think it's why I never visit their graves, it brings up the memories and I get very emotional. My grandmother lived for five years after we moved in. She was really going downhill at the end and I think we were all just waiting for her to go. Of course, I didn't really know what that meant at the time, having experienced so little death in my life up to that point.

As for my grandfather, he lived two years longer

than his wife. Looking back, it feels like much longer to me. Maybe my grandmother spent her last year in the hospital? I can't remember exactly. I know she died in the hospital after she had been there for many months. How many months, I don't know for sure. It was after she died that we got our first dog, Charlotte. I should point out that my grandmother's actual name was, my brother named our dog Lottie, not Charlotte, and that after one of his favorite childhood movies, Charlotte's Web. My parents saw the coincidence that Lottie is often a shortened form of the name Charlotte, but my brother and I had no idea at the time. I know my grandmother had not been fond of dogs, so my father had never had one as a child. We weren't sure how my grandfather would react, but it turned out he loved her just as much as we did. He would sit there in his swivel rocker with the remote, flicking channels until he found an old Western movie, and feeding Charlotte. Our dog got chubbier by the day, but she certainly ate well. Between my grandfather and our friends, I'm sure Charlotte ate more people food than dog food. She was a great dog. I've had a couple more dogs since I got a house of my own, but it seems no dog ever matches your first.

My grandfather grew more and more nervous after his wife passed away. I think it had something to do with us, his grandsons, growing up. I was in high school, driving and working. I know it bothered him when I came home late at night. The night he died, my mother told me he had been worried about me. When I got in that night, I checked in with him to show him that I was home safely. He went to sleep, but he never woke up the next day. I was at work when I got the call that he had died in his sleep. That was one of the worst phone calls I ever received.

My grandmother's sister, Evelyn, or "Auntie," and her husband, Jacko, lived next door to us. Through the years, I spent a lot of time visiting over at her house. She always had cookies and tea. Auntie and Jacko never had any children of their own. The funny thing was that I know she loved kids, so I have to assume there was another reason for it. Her husband, Jacko was a World War One veteran. Although he often seemed preoccupied, he was friendly enough. Their house always smelled like his pipe. Just thinking about it brings that tobacco smell right back to me. Pipe tobacco just seems to inject the atmosphere with the air of long lost memories. That's how it felt to me back then, anyway. I think my visits to Auntie grew even more nostalgic after my grandparents died. She would pull out photo albums, letters and other reminders of her earlier years. I wish I had even spent more time with her, but I was getting older, and doing the stuff that high school kids start doing. In high school, you start building a life that feels more adult to you, at least at the time. Still, you can never get those times with your elder relatives back, and even though I have fond memories of Auntie and Jacko, I wish I had more.

So, did my unusual experiences in that house start while my grandparents were still alive? Yes, I think they did. One thing I remember is a phenomenon I have come to learn is referred to as "shadow people." I would just about always have the feeling that I was being watched in that house. Many times I would see something, a black silhouette, just out of the corner of my eye, but when I would turn to look at it, it would be gone. Well, at least usually. There were a few times that I would turn and still see the silhouette, or the shadow, moving away from me for another second or two. Since I was a small child, I have been told what an over-active imagination I have, so I always chocked it up to that. I knew I was different and I knew people didn't get me, so I tried not to make too much out of the unusual things that I sometimes saw. I have watched monster movies on Creature Double Feature going back as far as I can remember, so I think my family always assumed my imagination was running wild.

Come to think of it, one of my earliest memories from before we even moved into Tucker's Court was of a shadow person coming straight at me, one night, while I was in my top bunk. My brother saw it, too. My dad played softball when we were younger, so he often came home after we were already in bed. I had seen the shape of a person outside the bedroom door and called out it, "Daddy?" The shape came into the room, moving straight towards me. It never said a word. As it approached, I expected more detail to come into focus and for it to become obvious that it was my dad. But no more details of the dark shape ever came into focus. It was getting closer, but it never became anything more than an approaching shadow. The figure moved towards me without making a sound. It even seemed to be surrounded in some sort of cloak of silence, if that makes any sense. I called out to it again, possibly several times, but got no response. Somehow I don't think my shouts, which my mother certainly should have heard and responded to, penetrated that aura of silence that surrounded the shadow man. I finally did what every little kid does in that situation; I dove under the covers and held them down tight. Nothing happened. Was it real? Did anything really happen? To this day, I don't know, but in the morning I woke up, still under the covers with the memory of the incident fresh on my mind. I later discussed what happened with my brother, who was on the bottom bunk. He confirmed that my voice had woken him up and he too had seen the shadowy figure approaching us. Like me, he felt great terror as it was almost upon us, and he hid under the covers. If it was a dream, or a nightmare, then it was one that was shared by my brother and me.

Okay, so that's my earliest memory of a shadow person. I was probably six or seven years old at the time. At least later, when I lived in my grandparent's home, the shadow people were just watching or moving away from me. None of those came right at me like that first one. Still, no one likes to be watched, and there was just always that feeling of being watched when I lived in that house. My brother and I each got our own room when we lived on Tucker's Court. It was nice to get that kind of freedom for the first time in my life, but let me tell you, there's safety in numbers. I was rarely comfortable in my room, alone at night. Almost every night I had to check in the closet and under the bed before I went to sleep. Even then, if I still felt like there was someone else in the room with me, I would just go to sleep with the lights on. Not a nightlight, mind you, but the room fully lit up. This happened more times than I can remember.

I never trusted the dark. As a matter of fact, even when I managed to shut the lights off, I usually fell to sleep with my eyes open, staring at the ceiling. I guess I didn't want anything sneaking up on me, while my eyes were closed. As I lied there on my back, I would see shapes swirling around in the darkness. If I stared long enough, the shapes would sometimes coalesce together and move towards me. This often got me to close my eyes and think maybe I was better off not seeing what flew about in the dark. I've always seen shapes and spots, even in the daytime. I have tinnitus, which is ringing in the ears as well. I think the strategy for dealing with these conditions is much the same; try to ignore it. If you can make your mind focus on other things, you can kind of forget about the ringing, or ignore the spots. It's when you really focus and pay attention to it that it can drive you crazy.

Years later, after my grandparents had died, I still could not shake the uncomfortable feeling of being watched. I have since found out that other people experienced the same feeling, especially when they were alone in the house. My father told me that while growing up in that house he would often sit with a baseball bat beside him, if he was alone. I also have a friend who spent a lot of time with us in that house, growing up. He has told me that he even left the house before, feeling that there was a presence that did not want him there. After my grandparents died, I would usually sit downstairs and read a book. Our dog, Charlotte, always lay down just below my armrest because I would reach down and pat her for hours, while I was reading. Sometimes I would just get the feeing there was someone looking over my shoulder and turn around. Of course, there was never anyone there. Charlotte seemed to also get those feelings, but it was also like she could see and hear things, that were just beyond my senses. Sometimes, Charlotte would kind of roll up at attention, and look over into a corner of the house at seemingly nothing. Her ears would perk up, the way they did when she was listening to you, for several minutes. Eventually her ears would go down and she would lie down again, waiting to be petted. If anything could make me more edgy than I already was, that was it.

It was a creaky house, too. At least, that's what my parents told me. Old houses have creaks. Yeah, right. The house I live in now is older than that house on Tucker's Court by about twenty years, and it doesn't nearly have the same kinds of odd sounds that I grew up with. My grandmother's room, before she became confined to the downstairs due to her hip, was directly over the living room. My grandmother loved her rocking chair and she would sit, knit, and rock for hours. The rocking chair motion gave off a particular creak of the floorboards that we all became accustomed to. Long after my grandmother was gone, we continued to hear that particular creaking of the floorboards over our heads, as we sat and watched television in the living room. "It's just the wind," my parents would say. One night, as I sat there with a couple of friends, "the wind" actually made the sound of footsteps. We knew no one was upstairs, so we ran up there to check it out. Naturally, there was nothing. It was just the wind, I suppose.

Other strange things happened from time to time. Once in a while, things would just go missing. I'm sure this happens to everyone, but do these things just re-appear in a place you have looked, dozens and dozens of times? I once lost a Stephen King book I was reading, the second book in The Dark Tower series. Now, I knew where I left this book. I always read in the same chair in the living room, while patting my dog Charlotte. Right next to this chair was a built-in bookcase where we kept the encyclopedias and a dictionary. If I was reading a book, I would always put it in that bookcase, so that it would be there when I sat down to read again. All I would have to do was reach over and pull it out. That book disappeared for about a year. One day, it was just gone. I searched and searched the house before finally giving up. As I was making plans to try to track down another copy (this was before the internet made it relatively easy to find collectibles), I went to that bookcase to grab the dictionary. What was sitting there, right beside the encyclopedias, as if it had never moved? My Dark Tower book, of course. I can't tell you how many times I looked in that exact same spot over the course of the year it was missing. Then, bang, like magic, it was right back where it should be.

One other time, I purchased tickets to take my girlfriend, who later became my wife, to see AC/DC in concert. About two weeks before the show, I realized the tickets were missing. I tore the house apart looking for them, but I could not find them in time for the show. We didn't go. Nowadays you could just show up at the ticket window with your confirmation email and credit card and have new tickets issued. I don't think you could do that back then. Anyway, a few weeks later, there the tickets were, sticking out from between two books in a book case, plain as day. How could they have been missed so many times? I don't know. It doesn't seem like they should have been, because it was so easy to see them when I found them. It was like they just reappeared out of thin air. It was like some entity was playing games with me.

I never wanted to be alone in that house, but of course, it happened all too often. Some of the scariest places in the house were the dark corners, of course. You know what I mean, right? The basement was a dimly lit, spider web filled dungeon. I read a short story once, which might have been by Frederic Brown, about some alien creature that crashed on earth and then proceeded to tunnel around, into people's basements. When the homeowners went down to investigate the strange noise, they would usually see the hole in the basement wall, just before the creature shot out some tentacle and killed them, or something like that. I read it a long time ago, but that is my recollection of it. I have always associated that story with that basement on Tucker's Court. I can't tell you how many times I ran up those narrow, too-steep stairs, trying to distance myself from some unseen terror lurking behind the Christmas decorations or a pile of old magazines.

The attic wasn't much better. It wasn't lit at all, so you could really only go up there in the daylight. There would however, be those times that my mother would send us up there for something or other after it was dark. My brother and I would go up, stupidly, with only one flashlight. You really needed two to pull off this job correctly, because one of us would keep shining the flashlight into those dark corners where you could swear you just heard something scratching. That would invariably leave the person who was looking for whatever my mother sent us up there for in complete darkness for a few terrifying moments. We'd yell at each other to bring the light back over. If I had to go it alone, I would just try to keep the beam focused on what I was searching for and ignore the little scratching sounds behind me and the feeling that someone was standing just over my shoulder, waiting for the perfect moment to reach down and scare the life out of me. Good times.

Personally, I never performed any type of séance or anything like that while I lived in that house. There was one time, however, that my brother and his friends used an Ouija Board down in the basement. Now, not all of what I heard about the incident seemed to agree, but the gist of it was this. They went down into the basement and set up their Ouija Board. It was homemade, I think, but I'm not sure about that. We didn't own the board game version, so if that was what they used, one of the friends must have brought it with them. Apparently, they made contact with a spirit. After asking it the usual teen-ager type of questions, the spirit started to give some instructions of its own. The spirit wanted my brother to hurt my father, and possibly himself. My brother ended up putting his hand through the glass on our front door and needing stitches. I remember being told that he put his hand through the window by accident, or in anger, or something like that. Eventually, the truth about what really happened came out. My mother followed that up by calling a priest to bless the house. I know we always had some holy water on hand after that incident.

I moved out of Tucker's court about six months before I got married, at age twenty-five. I was ready to get out on my own, and I think I'd had enough of that house. Even in my mid-twenties, I was still uncomfortable every time I was alone in the house. I was even beginning to wonder if I would ever outgrow my overactive imagination. My wife and I lived in a two family apartment with relatives of hers for a couple years before we bought a house of our own. I am proud to say that I actually did outgrow my over –active imagination, once I finally got away from that house. I have never had any experiences even close to resembling those that I grew up with on Tucker's Court. There have been no strange creaks, other than my son up in his room playing video games. I have seen no shadow people at my current residence. And despite the fact that I am a lover and collector of supernatural-type paraphernalia, I have not seemed to have attracted any restless spirits. It is pretty peaceful here.

My brother, on the other hand, bought that house on Tucker's Court from my mother. Good for him, he wanted it, but I never did. He's made a lot of changes to the old place, and it's really not recognizable as the house in which I grew up. I know a lot of that was his wife's doing, but I can't help wonder if he was just as eager to overhaul it and change the vibe of the place. How's it going for him now, you might ask? My brother's wife once saw the silhouette of a man in the window of his infant daughter's room. Sounds like one of the shadow people to me. At an early age, his younger daughter reported speaking to my long dead grandfather. My brother also admitted to me that he sometimes he feels a cold draft when he is in the middle of taking a hot shower, which is very disconcerting. His dog seems to sense something as well. This dog will often stand at the top of the stairs, shaking and refusing to go down to the first floor unless accompanied by a human. My college age niece also feels uneasy and has that sense of being watched when home alone in that house. I remember the feeling well. I don't know about weird creaks, but he has told me that to this day the television downstairs goes on and off with a mind of its own. I can't help but think of my grandfather, sitting in his swivel rocker, flicking channels and looking for an old Western. I miss you, gramps.

THE OLD MAN OF HOPTON
EMMA BUNN

When I was a little girl, my Dad looked for ghosts. Not under the bed or in the wardrobe like other Daddies did, but really look for ghosts!

He and a few friends had a group that researched and tried to find a real ghost or proof of one. While other Daddies played football or went fishing, they would pack up their equipment and would go off to haunted places for the night. People would contact them with their stories and sightings of anything unexplained or paranormal. Letters would arrive all the time and phone calls too. I didn't think this was anything different, there were always my Dad's bearded friends around and my Dad did a lot of writing. I don't think I realized that it was a bit different until I went to school!

None of this was ever hidden from me; I always knew what was going on. One of my favorite stories is of a ghost that was seen on a local duel carriageway of an old man that walked across the road at night and had caused crashes. It was only recently I realized just how many times that this ghost had been seen. Also almost all of the descriptions were the same of what the ghost looked like.

As I haven't actually seen this ghost myself, here are three of the full eye witness statements. I have changed all names but they are repeated here as they were written.

Mr. J was driving his Hillman Avenger car from Lowestoft to Yarmouth at approx 60 mph., when he

101

saw a 'mist' in front of him about 2 feet from the centre of the road into the slow lane. The mist then resolved itself into the figure of a man; he was tall, but with his shoulders 'hunched-over'. He had boots on which appeared to be tied around with string "like the Saxons" and was wearing a coat which came down to just below his knees. Regarding this coat, the witness says that as he got closer to the figure he could see that it was unlike an ordinary coat, and more like a cape, with many folds. The figure had long curly hair, which looked rather 'windswept' and unkempt. Although the man was staring directly at the oncoming car, the witness could not discern his features.

The figure was motionless in the road, and Mr. J had to break hard, upon doing so his car started to skid and he tried to correct it by applying the handbrake. The 'man' still made no effort to get out of the way, by which time the witness realized that there was nothing he could do to avoid hitting it. He involuntary closed his eyes for a second or so anticipating the impact, but when he opened them he was right on top of the figure and he was actually conscious of the car passing right through it "just like going through a cloud". At this point, he completely lost control of his vehicle, which slewed right round, went up onto the grass verge, and came to a stop facing in the opposite direction. The witness was unhurt although the rear axle of the car was damaged. A few seconds after stopping he climbed out of the car but there was nothing to be seen. He was initially angry about what had happened but later when he arrived at Yarmouth and thought about the incident he felt somewhat 'un-nerved'.

The witness claims to have no knowledge of the

reputed ghost here, save that the road is supposed to be 'haunted'.

There was no traffic in the vicinity at the time as far as he can recall. He later reported the incident to Lowestoft police.

Above information taken from an interview with witness at the scene of the incident at 14.45hrs November 3rd, 1981 — together with Mrs. H, a free lance journalist who was researching the story for Radio Norfolk.

And this one;

At just after 10pm on the evening of Wednesday April 4th 1987 Louise and her boyfriend John King of Lowestoft were driving home to Lowestoft from Great Yarmouth in his Hillman Avenger car.

They were driving along the A12 Hopton bypass behind a silver Metro when it suddenly swerved to avoid a figure standing about 2 meters onto the carriageway on the passenger (left-hand) side of the road, and in their headlights they could clearly see a figure standing in the road, it was this that the Metro had swerved to avoid.

The figure was that of a man wearing what appeared to be a long dark coat and seemed to be carrying something like a large bag in his hand. He was paying no attention to the traffic but simply staring straight ahead across the carriageway. He was slightly bent over and although the witnesses could not see his face, they noticed his mass of grayish-white, curly hair.

Louise said that she'd heard of the old man of Hopton sightings and accounts of the 'apparition' wearing 'big boots' and she looked at his feet to see if this man was wearing boots, but could not see his feet.

After they had driven passed Louise looked back could not see anything, but was unsure if this was because of the poor light or because he wasn't there.

She urged he boyfriend to turn the car round and check *if* the figure was still there but he didn't want to go back.

Taken from a telephone interview with Louise, aged 17, of Oulton Broad, Lowestoft.

And also this;

Mr. R Howard says that in the winter of 1957 (between January and April), he and a friend – Mr. R Jones of Lowestoft – were driving from Gt. Yarmouth to Lowestoft on the A12. They were in separate cars; Mr. Howard's being a Heinkel 'bubble' car. As they reached the stretch of road just to the south of the junction of the A12 with Jay Lane (OS 1in map 528988) they both saw a figure very similar to that described by Mr. C, cross the road in front of them from left to right. Mr. H stopped his car and turned round to get a better look at the figure, which was now very close and described it as a man wearing large boots, long fawn coat and a hat. The figure was very tall.

Mr. H says that both he and his friend were very frightened at the time – they did not see the figure disappear but realized that it was no longer there. Mr. H says that although there was nothing particularly odd about the appearance of the figure he says that he felt that there was something 'odd' about it. He also admitted to feeling very uneasy on this stretch of road both before and since this experience and even today avoids going this way if he can.

This took place between 22.00 hrs and midnight and the weather was wet and windy.

Mr. H says he did not see the article in the Lowestoft Journal concerning Mr. C's experience, he says that he received a telephone call from his friend Mr. Jones telling about the article that appeared in the Sunday Express on December 28th, 1980. Mr. H's reaction to Mr. C's description of what he saw and experienced was almost word for word his own experience.

And then all of these;

• In the autumn of 1937, a cyclist travelling this way from Lowestoft encountered a strange, stooped figure in the middle of the road a few hundred yards of Rackham's Corner at 2 a.m.

• Early in 1957, during the late evening, two men travelling in separate cars from Yarmouth to Lowestoft saw the figure of a man slowly cross the road in front of them close to Jay Lane. The figure "disappeared" upon reaching the other side. Both men were extremely frightened and disturbed by their experience.

• Christmas 1961 saw the untimely death of a 42-year old lorry driver whose fish lorry ploughed into a tree near Rackham's Corner for no apparent reason. The driver had earlier said that he had seen things on this stretch of road, and only a few months before his death had seen a 'grey mist' cross the road in front of his lorry. He travelled the road almost every day and always said that there was something "funny" about it.

• Christmas Eve 1977: Two women driving passed Hopton Post Office to Yarmouth saw the figure of a man standing on the side of the road, as their car drew level with it, he stepped out into the path of the car. The driver stood on the brakes but felt a bump as if they had hit him. Subsequent investigation revealed no sign of the old man. The driver was very distraught and upset by the incident.

• 1980, on November 23, police constable Phillip Green, driving to Lowestoft along the Hopton by-pass, saw a strange, hunched figure trudging across the road in front of his car. P.C. Green braked hard, but the figure had disappeared. His wife sitting beside him saw nothing.

• Three weeks later, on December 15, during the early evening, a couple in a Yarmouth-bound car on this same stretch of road, were forced to brake hard and swerve to avoid what appeared to be an old man slowly crossing the road in front of them. However, as the 'old man' appeared to take avoiding action when he saw the car, it is possible that there was nothing ghostly about him at all.

• December 2nd, 1981 a lady driver travelling to Yarmouth swerved to avoid "something" on the road near Hopton. In doing so the car left the road and the driver sustained injuries.

• Sometime during the summer of 1980, a young couple on a motorcycle encountered the 'old man' whilst driving along the Hopton by-pass one evening. They were also forced to take evasive action.

These are just a few of the many sighting seen on

this small stretch of road.

Then, one day whilst in the local record office with my Dad while he went through local records to see if there were any deaths that tied in with this ghost, he stumbled upon this, written here again word for word:

GORLESTON POSTMAN'S TRAGIC FATE
MARTYR TO DUTY AND CHRISTMAS WORK
MELANCHOLY INQUEST STORY

An inquest was held yesterday at the White House farmstead, Hopton upon the body of William Balls the rural postman, who was found dead on his rounds on a footpath running through a field at Hopton.

The Suffolk Coroner, Mr. C. W. Chaston, conducted the inquiry and there were present, on behalf of the Postal Authorities, Mr. L. S. Lugg (Postmaster of Yarmouth) and Mr. W.B. Cockrill (Sub-Postmaster of Gorleston). The body was viewed in a room adjoining that in which the inquest was held.

William Balls, the father of the deceased, a farmer residing at the White House Farm, said deceased was his son, aged 40. He was Rural Postman for the Hopton district and had been 22 years in the Postal Service. He had had fairly good health, but was subject to colds. Witness last saw him alive on Saturday night, on the road, when he was returning to his home in Gorleston, having gone his round. On Monday morning at 10.30, witness was called to deceased who had been found lying dead in witness's wheat field; about a ten minute walk from his home. There were several people around him and he had probably been dead about 2 hours. Blood and foam were issuing from his lips, and there was a pool of blood beside him Witness conveyed the body to his home. He had never known him to break a blood vessel before. He had not the slightest suspicion that deceased's death was other than natural. Deceased had had a bad cough all Christmas time, and he had no doubt that an attack of coughing caused him to break a blood vessel. There had been more work for deceased to do this Christmas than at any other time, and some mornings the weight had been more than he could carry. He had seemed as if he could hardly stand under the weight of his load, but on Monday morning, it did not seem so heavy as usual.

The Yarmouth Postmaster: "There is a Regulation that no Postman should carry more than 35 lbs, and that is not, according to the department, more than a man should carry".

Witness: "He had had more than he could carry. The sweat has poured off him sometimes when he put his parcels down and he seemed right done up".

"Do you know what the weight he had to carry was?" – "No, I never weighed it".

Arthur Halfnight, Postman, 249 Lowestoft Road, Gorleston, said he was well acquainted with the deceased and last saw him alive about 6 am on Monday in Gorleston Post Office. Deceased then appeared in his usual health, but was very quiet. Witness just touched his arm, and deceased said: "For God's sake don't pull me about". Witness thought that the deceased was feeling very queer then, but nothing more passed. Deceased was a very steady man. His load on Monday morning was "nothing out of the way". Witness had been too busy seeing after his own work to know whether deceased was over-loaded.

The Postmaster: "Did he make any complaint of being ill?"

Witness: "No".

The Postmaster: "Had he made any complaint, the sub-Postmaster would not have sent him off. He and every other postman know he is not compelled to carry more than 35 lbs. He should have declined to take it if he had any reason to think there was more than 35 lbs. That is well understood by every postman".

Robert Hales, Farm Laborer, Hopton, said that he last saw deceased alive at 6.30 on Saturday night walking towards Hopton on his round, when he seemed as usual. He could not say anything as to the weight deceased was carrying. On Monday morning, witness was ploughing near Mr. Ball's wheat field and when he reached the end of his furrow, he turned his head and saw something lying in the field. He went to the spot and found deceased lying downwards in a pool of blood. There were no marks of any struggle, and the deceased did not appear to have moved an inch. That was the way deceased would have gone to his father's house. Witness gave information of his discovery to Mr. Balls' son and the body was removed.

Dr. R. G. Bately said that he had attended deceased professionally off and on for the last 20 years, and on Saturday he called at witnesses Surgery. About 18 months since, deceased had 'flu, which left pneumonia. Since then a cavity had been forming in the left lung, and on Saturday he complained of a pain in, and said, "William, you must go home and rest yourself".

Deceased replied: "What am I to do? I must do my

duty".

Witness said: "You must go home and rest yourself or you will die suddenly one day". To that deceased answered that his work had been so heavy that he could not rest. He did not mention that he had been over-loaded. Witness said: "Your life depends upon yourself. If you keep at work, you will undoubtedly die. Come and tell me tomorrow if you intend to rest". Deceased did not come again to see him. From the external examination he had made of the body, and his knowledge of the deceased, he had not the slightest doubt death was due to a rupture of the blood vessel in the left lung. Deceased was not a strong robust man, but he was one of those men who had more pluck than strength and would not give up.

The Gorleston sub-Postmaster: "I don't think deceased carried more than the authorized weight. Of late, the work had increased considerably, and it was much greater than when he first took the duties. He had suffered late from fatigue."

The Coroner: "Have you reason to think that had been worked too much lately?" – "Yes".

"He had not complained?" – "No", but he appeared to me as though his work was too much for him. During the last 2 or 3 years, his work has been increased considerably. They applied for 2 deliveries at Hopton, and instead of making one round as he had done for the past 17 years; he has had to do 2 journeys. Since then, I thought deceased flagged considerably. When the second delivery was made in Hopton I think it was too much for him".

The Coroner: "Had he more than the average rural postman to do?" – "No, I think not, but it needs a strong robust man to keep that work up, as he had done for over 20 years. It was the second round that taxed him. Up to then deceased never ailed anything that I was aware of".

The Coroner: "As a matter of fact, you think that he had been hard worked lately?" – "I have always thought that the second delivery was too much to put upon him".

The Yarmouth Postmaster said he found in the official records that deceased had to cover in his round a distance of 16 miles and 2 furlongs, but that had been slightly reduced, so that the distance was now about 16 miles. The limit officially fixed for a rural postman was between 16 and 18 miles daily, so that 16 miles was not by any means considered to be a hard day's work. Deceased commenced at 6 am and worked until 9.30. He began again at 4.20 and finished at 6.30, so that he had between 5 and 6 hours work daily.

The Coroner: "A good deal would depend upon the weight carried?"

The Postmaster: "In no case would there be more than 35 lbs".

The Coroner: "There is no proof that he was carrying more on the day of his death".

Dr. Bately: "It might not be what he had to do on that day, but I should attribute a good deal of it to his extra work at Christmas time. He was not in a fit condition to do hard work. For a man in his weak condition it was too much".

The Coroner: "I should not mind the walk but not the 2 stone to carry".

The Postmaster: "He could have gone on sick leave, and have received full pay during the whole time of his absence if he had made any complaint whatever".

The Coroner: "He did not make any complaint apparently".

The Postmaster: "He was not solitary in that respect. Many postmen have worked when it would have been better for them to have given up for a day or two. Possibly it was so in this case".

The Coroner: "Do you consider Doctor, that his death was accelerated?"

Dr. Bately: "I can scarcely say accelerated. It may have been".

The Coroner: "It does not seem to be a question whether this death was accelerated by over-work at Christmas, bearing in mind that he was not a strong man, but he made no complaint to the Post Authorities. The Postmaster has told us fully what weight he had to carry, and what his duties were. I think that you will feel that for a strong, healthy man that would not have been too much. There is no need for the Jury to go into that question because the Doctor, though he thinks death may have been accelerated by over-work, does not go so far as to say so. I think if you return a verdict in accordance with the medical evidence you will go as far as the law requires.

The Jury then returned a verdict of "Death from the rupturing of a blood vessel", and handed their facilitations to the widow and family.

The Postmaster said that on behalf of the postal staffs at Yarmouth and Gorleston he desired to tender their deepest sympathy with the bereaved widow and family.

From the: Eastern Daily Press Wednesday 4/1/1899

My Dad couldn't believe it! Was this the ghost that

had been seen so many times walking across the main road? Could this postman still be trying to deliver his mail even after his death? We will never know. But even after all these years this ghost still pops up from time to time. In all his years of looking for ghosts thinks that this is the most likely one, especially so when a relative of William Balls read about this and sent my Dad a photograph of him, the first thing my Dad noticed? His mass of curly unkempt hair...

ABOUT THE AUTHORS

Kristina R. Mosley lives in Kensett, Arkansas. She believes she lives in a haunted house, but she has no definitive proof. Her work has been released in numerous publications, including *Flashes in the Dark*, *Hogglepot*, *Luna Station Quarterly*, *Evolutionary Blueprint*, and *Scifaikuest*. She blogs occasionally at kristinarmosley.blogspot.com, and she tweets too often at twitter.com/elstupacabra.

Lisamarie Lamb - Over recent years, I have written various short stories, plays, poems and novels in different genres, including romance and children's books. If you wish to see more examples of my writing, I have a blog in which I showcase flash fiction (www.themoonlitdoor.blogspot.com). But I believe that horror is where I am best.

I have self-published a horror novel, Mother's Helper, and a collection of short stories entitled Some Body's At The Door. I am also part of the anthologies Satan's Toybox: Demonic Dolls, Satan's Toybox: Toy Soldiers, Skeletal Remains, At The Water's Edge and The Old Sofa.

I have been accepted into nine more anthologies due to be released throughout 2012.

Tammy A. Branom started her writing career with true ghost stories in the *Haunted Encounters* anthologies, so when when the open submission call for *Tales from the Grave: An Anthology of True Ghost* Stories came up, she had to send in a story. She's been published both in print and online including *Flashes In The Dark*, *Fictitious Magazine*, *Ghost Magazine*, and numerous Static Movement anthologies. She is also am a columnist for *Unexplained Mysteries*. Check out her work at her website at: http://www.tammyabranom.com/

Paul S Huggins has been a fan of horror since an early age. He has now made the momentous decision to impart his darkest most terrifying thoughts and ideas to paper. Paul hails from the United Kingdom within the witchcraft rich county of Suffolk, and resides there with his Wife, two daughters and a familiar. Paul would say zombies are in his blood, but thankfully he is still living.

Melinda Derfler - Born in 1959 in Lombard, Illinois, Melinda met and married the neighbor's son, James Derfler in 1978. She has worked in the publishing field since 1986 in positions from Publisher's Assistant to Sales Manager. Widowed in October 2008, she left the office world, and opened her own pet grooming business, *Your Place or Mine*, in February 2010. She has played piano from age eight until present, she is a non-professional singer, a trained automotive mechanic, has a degree in Landscape Design and Horticulture, as well as Pet Grooming and Animal Behavior. She currently lives with her three dogs in both Lombard and Antioch, Illinois, one house of which is still spiritually active.

John Irvine was born in Lower Hutt, New Zealand in 1940, but travelled widely in Australia and Papua New Guinea thereafter for 29 years. John lives with his blonde writer/poet wife in Colville on New Zealand's picturesque Coromandel Peninsula and occasionally lets his dark side out to play with the terrified local sheep. His website can be seen at: www.cooldragon.co.nz where you may find links to his various publications.
Favourite band: Captain Matchbox Whoopee Band

David Price studied Creative Writing at Salem State College. For more than twenty-five years he has worked in the family hardwood floor business. He lives in Peabody, Massachusetts with his wife and two children. "Tuckers Court" is his first published story.

Emma Bunn was born to hippy parents in the 70s. Raised in Lowestoft, Suffolk on literary diet of things that go bump in the night, she has always enjoyed writing. She is a Mother, Librarian and mad cat lady.

ABOUT THE EDITOR

R.G. Nojek lives in Illinois with his eighty- seven your old father. He enjoys a scary true ghost story as much as the next person. In addition, has been writing and reading them since his early teens.

COPYRIGHT

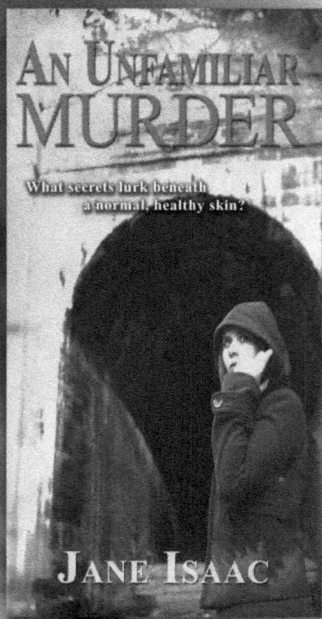

www.ingramcontent.com/pod-product-compliance
Lightning Source LLC
Chambersburg PA
CBHW050530280326
41933CB00011B/1536